Roy Blount, Jr.

Twayne's United States Authors Series

Frank Day, Editor

Clemson University

TUSAS 567

Roy Blount, Jr.
Photographed by Christopher Little.

Roy Blount, Jr.

By Jerry Elijah Brown

Auburn University

Twayne Publishers
A Division of G. K. Hall & Co. • *Boston*

90-821

Roy Blount, Jr.
Jerry Elijah Brown

Copyright 1990 by G. K. Hall & Co.
All rights reserved.
Published by Twayne Publishers
A division of G. K. Hall & Co.
70 Lincoln Street
Boston, Massachusetts 02111

Excerpts from *Webster's Ark/Soupsongs* by Roy Blount, Jr., © 1987 by
Roy Blount, Jr., reprinted by permission of Houghton Mifflin Company.

Copyediting supervised by Barbara Sutton.
Book production by Janet Z. Reynolds.
Book design by Barbara Anderson.
Typeset by Compset, Inc., Beverly, Massachusetts.

First published 1990.
10 9 8 7 6 5 4 3 2 1

The paper used in this publication meets the minimum requirements
of American National Standard for Information Sciences—Permanence
of Paper for Printed Library Materials, ANSI Z39.48-1984. ∞™

Printed and bound in the United States of America.

Library of Congress Cataloging-in-Publication Data

Brown, Jerry Elijah, 1945–
    Roy Blount, Jr. / by Jerry Elijah Brown.
        p.   cm.—(Twayne's United States authors series ; TUSAS 567)
    Includes bibliographical references and index.
    ISBN 0-8057-7609-5
    1. Blount, Roy—Criticism and interpretation.   I. Title.
II. Series.
PS3552.L687Z57   1990
818'.5409—dc20   90-36797
                                                                            CIP

For Libby

Contents

About the Author

Jerry Elijah Brown is four years younger than Roy Blount, Jr., and is, like Blount, a journalist and a Southerner. He was raised on a farm in Clarke County, Alabama, and attended Auburn University, where he majored in journalism, minored in English and agriculture, and edited the student newspaper, the *Auburn Plainsman.* He earned an M.A. degree in creative writing from Hollins College in 1968 and a Ph.D. degree in English from Vanderbilt University in 1974. From 1976 to 1979 he was editor of the *Vinton Messenger,* a weekly newspaper near Roanoke, Virginia. Since 1979, he has been a professor of journalism at Auburn University, and from 1988 to 1990 he was Humanities Scholar-in-Residence at the Auburn University Center for the Arts and Humanities. He is the editor of *Clearings in the Thicket: An Alabama Humanities Reader* and is coauthor of *The Federal Road through Georgia, the Creek Nation, and Alabama.* His essay on Roy Blount's humor appears in *The Vanderbilt Tradition: Essays in Honor of Thomas Daniel Young.*

Preface

This book is written for those who enjoy the work of Roy Blount, Jr., those who are curious about the life of a contemporary writer who earns his living by his wit, and those who are interested in modern humor generally. As the last decade of the twentieth century begins, Blount is one of the nation's best-known—and best—literary humorists, one who is providing a portrait of the times that, for mysterious reasons not explained in this book or any other, we laugh at. To approach the work of a contemporary writer who is so prolific that by the time this volume is published another book by him probably will have appeared has required the kinds of assistance common to biography, rather than to literary study.

Accordingly, the first acknowledgment, which should also be the ne plus ultra of praise for a humorist, goes to Roy Blount, Jr., for writing that not only continues to be funny even after it is explicated and examined but also inspires curiosity about the works and the writer. I am especially grateful to Roy for letters and telephone conversations that reveal his life and his living and for granting me access to his store of reviews, interviews, audiotapes, and personal papers. Thanks to his assistance, this book, which is not intended as a biography, can provide insight into the life of a contemporary author whose livelihood depends on what he writes.

In no order of priority, the following are also thanked for their help: Susan Blount, for talking about her brother and their family; Thomas Daniel Young, for advising me to consider the work of his former student; James M. Cox, for his personal advice and exemplary prose; Lorretta Need and Diane Hunter of the *Atlanta Journal-Constitution,* for access to personnel records and newspaper files; Marice Wolfe and Joan Sibley of the Special Collections Department of the Jean and Alexander Heard Library of Vanderbilt University, for documents detailing Blount's student writings; Rosalie Miller of Minnesota Public Radio, for information on Blount's days with Garrison Keillor on "A Prairie Home Companion"; David Alsobrook of the Carter Presidential Library, for bibliographical assistance; Sally Ann Berk of Villard Books, for a galley-book, and Jim Jermanok of International Creative Management, for a videotape of Blount on "The Tonight Show"; Kyle

David Young, deputy director of the Country Music Foundation, for artfully and swiftly locating obscure song lyrics; Reese Cleghorn, dean of the University of Maryland College of Journalism, for recalling his days with Blount in the editorial department of the *Atlanta Journal*; and Frank Day of Clemson University, for sympathetic and sensible editing.

Nearer to home, Glenn Anderson, Barbara Bishop, Mary Rankin, and Marcia Boosinger of the Humanities Department of the Ralph Brown Draughon Library of Auburn University have been tireless and cheerful trackers of fact; for them this acknowledgment is as inadequate as it is earnest. The direction provided and errors prevented by Caine Campbell, Ward Allen, and Bert Hitchcock, reliable scholars and trusted friends, place the author of this book even deeper in their debt. Without the steady support of Leah Atkins, Cathy Badura, Jay Lamar, and Serlester Williams, colleagues at the Auburn University Arts and Humanities Center who never even questioned why anyone would undertake the strange task of writing about humor, this book would never have been continued. With a special note of gratitude and affection, I add that without the forbearance of Libby, Brooks, and Lindsay Brown it would never have been completed.

Completed, of course, but not complete. Because this book catches Roy Blount, Jr., in medias res, it merely surveys his production through 1990—and not all of his production at that. Writings that best represent his development, his interests, and his techniques have been selected, which means that a given reader's favorite essay might be excluded. Viewed as a whole, Roy Blount's writing is strong, with the promise of becoming stronger still, and his joint reputations as literary humorist and popular entertainer are growing, in tandem and at equal rates. Though I hope Roy Blount's profound and funny writing is far from finished, I know that it is significant enough even now to merit this work of appreciation.

Jerry Elijah Brown

Auburn University

Chronology

1941   Roy Alton Blount, Jr., born 4 October in Indianapolis, Indiana, where his parents, Roy and Mattye Louise Floyd Blount, had recently moved from Jacksonville, Florida.

1943   Moves with family to Decatur (DeKalb County), Georgia.

1955   Moves with family to Dallas, Texas, and back to Decatur, Georgia.

1959   Writes sports column for the *Decatur-DeKalb News*; is senior class president; receives Grantland Rice Sportswriting Scholarship to Vanderbilt.

1961   Summer work with the *Morning Telegraph* in New York.

1963   Editor of the *Vanderbilt Hustler*; membership in Phi Beta Kappa; graduates with major in English from Vanderbilt and wins Woodrow Wilson Fellowship at Harvard.

1964   Earns M.A. in English from Harvard; marries Ellen Pearson; enters U.S. Army, stationed at Governors Island, New York.

1966   Daughter Ennis born; moves to Decatur, Georgia; is reporter for the *Atlanta Journal*.

1967   Becomes editorial writer and op-ed columnist for the *Atlanta Journal*; teaches freshman English part-time at Georgia State University.

1968   Moves to New York and is staff writer for *Sports Illustrated*. Son John born.

1972   Divorced.

1974   *About Three Bricks Shy of a Load*; poem published in the *New Yorker*.

1975   Leaves *Sports Illustrated*; moves to Mill River, Massachusetts; becomes free-lance writer.

1976   Marries Joan Ackermann; is contributing editor and sports columnist for *Esquire*.

1980   *Crackers*.

1981   First appearance on "A Prairie Home Companion."

1983   Contributing editor and sports columnist for the *Atlantic*; *One Fell Soup*.

1984   *What Men Don't Tell Women*.

1985   *Not Exactly What I Had in Mind*.

1986   *It Grows on You*.

1987   *Soupsongs/Webster's Ark*.

1988   "Roy Blount's Happy Hour and a Half" performed at American Place Theatre.

1989   *Now, Where Were We?*; divorced.

1990   *First Hubby*.

Chapter One

The Humor of
Roy Blount, Jr.:
An Overview

Si legetis, scribam. ["If you will read it, I will write it."]
    —letterhead on the personal stationery of Roy Blount, Jr.

A hundred years ago no one predicted that Mark Twain would emerge from a pack of journalists, humorists, and comedians as one of the principal figures of American life. He was a popular writer and entertainer, and even though his work was recognized within his own lifetime as a cut above that of his peers, it was not until *Huckleberry Finn* came to be regarded as a singular literary and historical achievement—Ernest Hemingway considered it the wellspring of modern American literature—that Mark Twain began to gain the academic homage he never needed and never sought. As this book goes to press, Roy Blount, Jr., is perhaps at the top—though who can presume?—of a popular literary career that strikingly resembles that of Mark Twain and other literary comedians of the last half of the nineteenth century. Blount's writings have been published, by his count, in almost a hundred different periodicals and almost fifty general anthologies. He is the author of nine books, with another collection planned. He has also completed a successful one-man off-Broadway show and appears often on national television programs and in lecture halls across the country. To compare Blount to the literary humorists and comedians who thrived throughout most of the last century is not to overlook the dark side of the analogy: many decades after the great successes of Josh Billings, Artemus Ward, and Petroleum V. Nasby, their works are rarely read and few but scholars know what their real names were. Nevertheless, to remark on the rise of Mark Twain's reputation as a way of approaching Blount's writing is to remind oneself that popular writing is not, by necessity, ephemeral and subliterary.

Like Samuel Clemens, Blount started as a newspaperman and went to the East to make a name for himself as a magazine journalist; he moved from reporter and editorialist on the *Atlanta Journal* to staff writer for *Sports Illustrated,* developing such a distinctive style that the sensibility of the writer eventually surpassed the importance of the subject. However he has earned his living, Blount has engaged in humor; in fact, he has been a humorist since his high school days, and his straightest prose reflects the sensibility of his humor. By 1981, after Blount had published two widely acclaimed books and had begun to appear with Garrison Keillor on the popular National Public Radio program "A Prairie Home Companion," it was apparent that the persona in his essays had emerged as a character, a literary performer using the techniques and style developed on the printed page, and it was almost impossible thereafter to avoid comparing him with others who practiced literary humor both in print and on the stage.

If Blount's career fits the pattern of the nineteenth-century literary comedians, among them Charles Farrar Browne (Artemus Ward), David Ross Locke (Petroleum V. Nasby), and Henry Wheeler Shaw (Josh Billings), all of whom were both humorists and literary comedians, both writers and stage performers, it also approximates the careers of their twentieth-century counterparts, among them Will Rogers and, of late, Mark Russell. The tendency in most recent newspaper humorists and stand-up comedians, however, has been toward political commentary compressed into verbal cartoons, editorial paragraphs, and one-liners, not toward the broader social humor, expressed in sketches, essays, and light verse, that marked the nineteenth-century humorists. That Roy Blount, Jr., should succeed along the lines of the first humorists/comedians without appearing to trade on their tradition, even as camp, is one comment on his particular genius and on the state of literature in our times.

To compare Blount's work to that of the nineteenth-century literary comedians is merely to swell a progress. Blount's writing has been so diverse in its forms and staggering in its volume that it is difficult not to conclude that all the traditions of American humor converge in one writer. As a Southerner educated in the literary humor of his region and aware of its continuities, Blount draws on the earliest frontier literature, the Old Southwest humor developed by his fellow Georgian Augustus Baldwin Longstreet, Johnson Jones Hooper of Alabama, George Washington Harris of Tennessee, and others who introduced vernacular narration, combined the voices of educated and uneducated speakers, and juxtaposed refinement and rawness—and who, in so doing, set the stage for Mark Twain. Blount may also be compared to the more recent newspaper humorists—to Russell Baker, Dave Barry, Erma Bombeck, Art Buchwald, and Lewis Grizzard—though his writing exceeds the subject and space limitations of the newspaper column. As a sportswriter, he is compared to George Plimpton and Dan Jenkins, and his expository magazine prose is regarded as a model of the type. His essays in *Rolling Stone* and *Esquire* invite comparisons with those of Hunter Thompson, Tom Wolfe, and other New Journalists, who use the techniques of prose fiction to depict fact. Blount is also one of a new school of literary humorists that includes, among many others, Veronica Geng, Calvin Trillin, Ian Frazier, and Frank Gannon. Blount himself has always seen his work against the great tradition of modern American humor—the *New Yorker* and Algonquin writers, a pantheon that includes Dorothy Parker, Alexander Wolcott, S. J. Perelman, James Thurber, and Robert Benchley, his earliest role model.

To establish connections, of course, is not really to say what makes Blount's writing funny. If a theory of humor is evident in Blount's writing, it is as old as that of Aristotle and Thomas Hobbes, who held, from varying perspectives, that what we find funny issues from a sense of incongruities.[1] Relating incongruities on the deepest and most abstract level to his own work, Blount writes that humor "springs from a certain desperation, which uses jujitsu on looming fear and shame, flirts almost pruriently yet coolly with madness and sentimentality, and fuses horse sense with dream logic."[2]

Yet despite this abiding sense of incongruity, Blount remains a humorist, not a satirist; he looks for reconciliations; and his circumspect, subjective criticisms rarely draw blood. Though the intellect evident in Blount's powers of logic, his quick grasp of guiding abstractions, and his wide reading set him apart as a literary humorist (as do his command of language and his use of literary techniques), his humor retains a boyish quality—again, not unlike Mark Twain's. At once adult and adolescent, his writing demonstrates the qualities of "cultured insolence," which in Blount's writing might be redefined as an "exuberant irreverence," that Aristotle considered a characteristic of the young.[3] But beyond remarking on the incongruities, explicating texts, and describing techniques, little in the way of deeper analysis is possible—not because Blount's humor is shallow but because, as the reviewers indicate, it exhibits a salient property of humor: it resists critical analysis. Even if it did so submit, an analysis would be mocked by the liveliness and readability of the humor, or the humor would be ruined. As a boy growing up in Georgia, Blount read in the 1941 humor anthology assembled by E. B. and Katharine S. White, "Humor can be dissected as a frog can, but the thing dies in the process and the innards are discouraging to any but the scientific mind."[4]

Though Blount's humor resists critical analysis, it cannot be dismissed. At its best, it is obviously more than a document and more than occasional journalism written by a commercial writer. Yet the temptation in studying humor is to elevate it to the level of a literary genre, especially to nudge it toward satire or "social commentary." Blount's humor inspires comparisons not because it is derivative, though it does evoke the work of others, but because comparing seems either the first way or the only way to evaluate the humor. The compulsion of book reviewers to use comparisons to praise—only rarely to condemn—Blount's humor is evidence of the general inability to analyze a collection of humorous pieces as if it were a novel or some other specific genre. Newspaper and magazine reviewers often seek out comparisons as a way of elevating the humor, but, though humor is widely studied, the scholarly consensus is that it is low, amorphous, and not worthy of the attention given to "serious" literature. Despite the genius in humor, the talent of the writer, and the power of the work to please, the inability to get a firm grip on humor is often enough to prompt wonder as to why one with the gift of humor writing would persist in producing literature destined to remain outside the academic pale. A classic example of the academic grievance against the lowness of humor is expressed by Joseph Epstein, in his reflection on the life of S. J. Perelman, who "never surmounted the confusion in his life, at least not in his writings. His comic response to life gave many people pleasure, which is no small blessing. Still, one cannot help thinking that, had things worked out differently, he might have been an American Evelyn Waugh. Instead, wanting in ambition or soul or the energy necessary for art, he had to settle for being a humorist."[5]

Not wanting in ambition, soul, or energy, Roy Blount, Jr. has settled for being a humorist. In his first twenty years of professional writing he has shown that humor can be, to use one of his phrases, a level on which issues can be resolved—not the only level, to be sure, and if not resolved in the sense of permanently settled then at least given a preliminary hearing. The "level of humor," most often thought of as low, can as easily be considered high; it may be more than a trivial response, and it may even be the first or the best level at which to consider some matters—for instance, the presidencies of Jimmy Carter and Ronald Reagan. No person who thinks about the bizarre and troubling nature of Carter's four years will dismiss Blount's *Crackers* as low and mean, and no one who scrutinizes what Reagan represents will consider Blount's astute observations in *Now, Where Were We?* and in his *Spy* crossword puzzles merely partisan.

In his explorations of the major concerns of the age, Blount often confronts feelings about issues and the mindless way in which they are expressed, and, in so doing, creates for himself and his readers a freedom from self-righteousness and cant. In its approach to received attitudes about race, for example, Blount's humor can reduce right and left; though he is a liberal Democrat and though his biases are apparent, he needles Georgia segregationist governor Lester Maddox and black Olympian Carl Lewis with equal fervor. Blount also sees the large in the small. When he writes about football in America, the fads in hair care, and coping with technology, he is doing more than elevating the trivial or the trying; he is providing a way to understand and to respond to elements that have become, for better and for worse, essential to our lives. When he takes on such a controversy as the shifting role of gender in contemporary America, he is showing what risks humor must take. In addition to whatever else it may do, Blount's humor establishes its own level of reality and offers the reader a liberated sensibility—blessed relief from the old—that is accepted because the perspective of the humorist exposes an unrecognized truth and the language of the humorist provides a fresh, valid way of expressing it. Readers get pleasure, but they also gain a new insight and, with it, a chance to participate in the humorist's freedom.

That we live and read (if we do read) in a time when readers capable of being piqued by concern are often urged toward the dull, the strident, and the abstract—confusing these with the profound—rather than toward the entertaining and the concrete may be another reason Blount's humor is popular. It is counterliterature, occasionally cheeky, often brilliant, and always freewheeling, but it does not surrender the field of examination to supposedly higher forms of expression. Blount is aware of the liberties inherent in the lowly state of humor, in particular the access to readers it provides. In assuming the role of humorist, Blount is aware of the task and the risk: he must impress and convince readers that he is defining and confronting important issues rather than avoiding them and that he has a sensibility capable of dealing with what has been confronted. If he succeeds he will have created his audience, and that audience will embrace the humorist's perspective and insight. The low and mundane—like humor, easily overlooked as significant—will be seen in a new light, and the loftiest of people and concepts will be brought to the humorist's and the readers' level. The humorist will be honored for what he has given; his wit will be quoted, his books bought, and his presence sought after.

Judged by these admittedly fluid and general critical and social standards, Roy Blount, Jr., is obviously succeeding; he has risen in stature as a pure humorist, maintaining all the tensions inherent in his craft and producing literature that brings pleasure even after the laughter. For students interested in Roy Blount, Jr., and modern American humor, the chapters that follow show how his career has developed, what he has written and performed, and how his work joins the mainstream of American literary humor.

Chapter Two
Person and Persona

And although there is a disharmony in comedy that causes us to
worry a bit, as well as to laugh, there is also something expansive
and vital with which comedy is harmonious. Although there is dis-
cord, somehow things aren't really amiss, and in a way they are even
sublime.
   —Roy Blount, Jr., from an essay on George Bernard Shaw (1963)

This guy was on his way to being the leading humorist in the
country.
   —Reese Cleghorn

From Cradle to College: 1941–59

The persona in the writing of Roy Blount, Jr., and the speaker by
the same name on radio, television, and stage are projections of a
bright Southern boy who made up his mind early to be a humorist.
Blount was brought up in an affluent suburb in the postwar South by
intelligent, largely self-educated parents who had risen to success from
working-class backgrounds. Often identified as a native of Decatur,
Georgia, he was, in fact, born to Roy and Mattye Louise Floyd Blount
on 4 October 1941 in Indianapolis, Indiana, where his father was em-
ployed by the canned goods division of Libby Foods. As their son remembers the family history, both parents had attended Andrew
Jackson High School in Jacksonville, Florida, but they actually met
after graduation at Main Street Methodist Church. They acted in
church plays, attended Nelson Eddy–Jeanette MacDonald movies, and
married during the Great Depression. Roy was a native of Hosford, in
the Florida panhandle, and Louise was born in Monticello, Mississippi,
the daughter of a railroad worker. Orphaned, she was moved from one
relative to another until she went to Jacksonville to live with her aunt
by marriage, Pearl Floyd, whose husband-to-be had come calling after
reading her column in a railroad newspaper. The great-aunt became a
bedridden member of the Decatur household and died when Roy, Jr.,
was about three. He remembers standing by her bed for hours listen-

ing, though he does not recall her stories. Mrs. Blount told her son
that one of her forebears, John Y. Floyd, wrote a political novel entitled
The Opening of a Chestnut Burr, and a female cousin wrote *Bound by
Honor's Chains,* a novel that was stolen from her "by a city slicker (who
was not bound by honor's anything) and published under his name."
Mrs. Blount also believed her family was distantly related to Robert
Frost "through a ghostly branch of the family she referred to as the
Von Sweringers."[1]

From Indianapolis the Blounts were transferred to Columbus,
Ohio—where they did not run into any Thurbers, the son says—and,
when Roy, Jr., was two, to Decatur, in DeKalb County, then a suburb
and now a part of metropolitan Atlanta. Blount worked in the sales
division of Packard; early in 1955, when Roy, Jr., was in the eighth
grade, his father was transferred to Dallas. The family, which now
included a daughter, Susan, a first-grader, did not like Dallas; the
Blounts were happy to return to Decatur before the next school term
started. When the Packard was discontinued, Blount took a job mar-
keting the Edsel; although that make followed the Packard into history, he was "never apologetic" about being twice associated with
obsolescence, but he was displeased with the Ford corporation. For a
year after the demise of the Edsel, he sold real estate; then he entered
the savings and loan business, where he quickly succeeded.[2] Indeed,
he became president of Decatur Savings and Loan and a prominent
figure in both the national thrift organization and area civic affairs. He
served as chairman of the Decatur Board of Education and is remembered as a pioneer in the effort to improve urban transportation. For
six years, he served on the board of the Metropolitan Atlanta Mass
Transit Authority (MARTA), which he called the "greatest thing that's
ever happened in Atlanta."[3] In 1972, when he stepped down as chairman of the MARTA board, he made a point of criticizing the Atlanta
newspapers through a period that included his son's two years as a
reporter and editorial writer: "Bite your tongue when the newspapers
get after you," he was reported as saying. "They do not report our story
accurately or completely and then from there the editorial writers take
those incomplete and inaccurate stories and write their opinions about
them from their ivory towers."[4] Blount became chairman of the board
of *Atlanta Magazine,* owned by the Atlanta Chamber of Commerce, of
which he was also a board member, shortly before he died of a heart
attack at age sixty in April 1974.[5] The editorial page of the Atlanta
morning newspaper called his death "truly a great loss. . . . Mr.

Blount was a soft-spoken and friendly man, but he maintained a firm strength in his beliefs and his integrity was unquestioned. Humanity could use more of his kind."[6]

The father's contributions to the son's writing are referred to in the essay entitled "Jrs.," in *Crackers*:

My father and I took intimate if qualified pride in each other, were told we *moved* alike, were mistaken for each other on the phone; but I rarely felt that I had pleased my father and myself, or that he had pleased himself and me, with one stroke. Which may be why I hardly ever do anything with one stroke. . . .

My father *made* me a Bunsen burner once. Just out of the blue. I want to mention that. And at the time I *needed* a Bunsen burner.[7]

Asked about his father, Blount told one interviewer, "He had a sort of large, dignified presence. I wonder about what fathers ought to do for their sons. But one thing he did was he cut a broad swath. I had this sense that a person in my family could loom large if he wanted to. There was a kind of distance between us. I always wished we had more conversations. We never had any heart-to-heart talks, but my father was great at sensing my direction and then getting out of the way."[8]

Louise Blount apparently had the more direct and immediate literary influence on her son. She figures as a character in one of his on-stage anecdotes as the teetotaling Methodist mother, anxious about appearances, who drags the teenage Roy to the liquor store where she hopes to buy a single can of beer for setting Susan's hair. Blount dedicated *Crackers* to her (also to his second wife and to his two children by the first marriage) with the inscription "And to my mother, who taught me how to read in Georgia." In a 1984 *Boston Globe* interview, Blount alluded to his mother's influence. "One of the things that made me a writer was having 'Brer Rabbit' read to me at an early age," he said, "because it captured the sound of the way people talked."[9] (Blount wrote his own version of an Uncle Remus fable, "How Miss Wren Stood in De Do'," when he was a columnist for the *Atlanta Journal*, after he learned that "The Wren's Nest, Joel Chandler Harris's home, was being maintained as a museum for whites only." The column is reprinted in *One Fell Soup*.)[10]

Susan Blount remembers her mother as a woman with a sharp sense of irony and the ability to make ordinary events into stories; she also incorporated incidents into a family history. A phonograph record of young Roy singing "God Bless America"—an ironic start for a man who calls himself "singing impaired"—was made on a machine at a friend's house and kept around the family for years.[11] Louise Blount also recognized herself as a Southern version of the Jewish mother, not above manipulating with guilt. According to Susan, the persona often projected in her brother's humor—"a frustrated, conflicted person" who has to bear more responsibility than is possible or fair—is the product of Mrs. Blount's influence. At home, scenes were avoided, and the children did not talk back.[12]

Blount's humor, generally, and his talent for stage performance are related to his mother's influence. "She dramatized herself, not without grounds, as intolerably burdened," he wrote in a personal letter. "She suffered a great deal from arthritis during my childhood, but there was more than that: I inherited from her a sense of unspecified woe, a desire to recognize and alleviate woe, to work through woe."[13] She taught her son such recitations as "Foolish Questions" and "Life Gits Tee-jus, Don't It?," the latter a white-dialect poem.[14] The happy response Blount received when he recited the sorrowful poem for his grammar school assembly and his mother's Sunday school class completed a formative experience that was connected with the humor he would write, the religion he would reject, and the deep background of his family:

Cheer out of hopelessness. My mother's despair foisted on me but leavened in this bizarre way. I shouldn't say foisted—you can't help passing things like that on (and hell, life's like that substantially anyway ain't it?) and if you can pass it on with adaptive skills it's a gift. I was supposed to learn religion too, along those lines, but I couldn't see that religion worked as well for my mother as she wanted me to believe it did, and after a while it didn't work for me, I was sure of that, because it was too much tied up in the repression that went with fear instead of the uplift that was supposed to transform it. I'm not saying there wasn't any uplift in the religion, but to me it was too much bound up with anti-intellectualism. But humor didn't have to be anti-intellectual and repressive; humor could make you think and jump. The old-time religion made you jump, but that impulse was being left behind by the modern white Methodist church. I have dim recollections of religion being deeply rousing, back in the days when we called the preacher Bro. instead of Rev. or Dr.

"Foolish Questions" was in a similar mode.

The contrast between "Life Gits Teejus" and my parents' almost feverish industry—which left them tired and cranky and guilt-inducing—is striking,

I think. Also of course we're getting into hillbilly or white trash stereotypes here, and fatalism. I think a lot of what I write arises from "Life Gits Tee-jus." Some day I would like to work all these connections out.[15]

Louise Blount had a cancerous eye removed when she was pregnant with Susan and wore a glass eye, of which she was always conscious. She died of cancer in 1981, at age sixty-six.[16]

The writing talents of Roy Blount, Jr., were recognized early. At Decatur High School he wrote for the *Scribbler* and covered high school sports for the community paper, the *Decatur-DeKalb News.*[17] Though he had come to terms with the sad truth that, wherever he went to college, he would never be a "three-sport immortal," he was visited early by events that would eventually figure in happy ironies. When he was twelve, his father gave him a copy of *Bury Me in an Old Press Box,* by *Nashville Banner* sports editor Fred Russell, and suggested that Roy consider being a "sports*writer.*" When he was thirteen, he read the autobiography of Grantland Rice, the writer of stylized sports prose remembered for naming the Four Horsemen of Notre Dame, for penning the verse "When the One Great Scorer comes to write against your name— / He marks not that you won or lost but how you played the game," and for serving as mentor to the Babe Ruth of sportswriters, Red Smith. One of Blount's high school English teachers, Ann Lewis, convinced him that he "could write a certain kind of workable thing."[18] (In the acknowledgments to *One Fell Soup* Blount wrote that but for Ann Lewis he "would probably be an astrophysicist or some damned thing. Part of 'Chickens' comes from a theme I wrote for her in the tenth grade.")[19]

The irony began to emerge when he applied for, and won, a four-year scholarship to Vanderbilt, named for Rice with Russell as one of the judges. (The scholarship, funded by the Thoroughbred Racing Association, is now named for both Vanderbilt alumni.) Blount professes not to know why he got the prestigious scholarship, but he appreciates the pattern of coincidences. "If things had kept falling into place that way, I would by now have made everybody *forget* Grantland Rice. And Ring Lardner. And Elvis," he said. Getting the scholarship was almost like "being spotted and signed by a baseball scout."[20] To accept the scholarship, Blount had to turn down a full National Merit Scholarship, which he had won over 174,000 other applicants. For all his interest in sports and sportswriting, however, he had another vocation on his mind. On the Grantland Rice scholarship application he said his ambition was to be a "humorist and bon vivant like the late Robert Benchley."[21]

The Vanderbilt Years: 1959–63

Though the scholarship Blount earned was intended to encourage students inclined toward sportswriting, Vanderbilt University has no school or department of journalism. Blount chose to major in English and to write news, not sports, for the *Vanderbilt Hustler,* the campus weekly. Entering in late September 1959, he reported first on the chancellor's remarks at the delayed freshman convocation and noted that the speaker promised to speak for twelve minutes, instead of the customary six, but "then attacked the subject with a vigor that presaged a commencement talk of at least 24 minutes"; the chancellor charged the class of '63 to strive for a broad education if it wished "to escape being swamped by the Russians."[22] At college less than a month, Blount was writing front-page lead stories; during his second semester, he began to cover important beats—the Student Senate and the Interfraternity Council—and to report on events related to the most noteworthy phenomenon on Southern college campuses during the early 1960s, the civil rights movement.

Blount wrote about the Student Senate's support of the administration's ouster of a black graduate student in the divinity school who had participated in Nashville sit-ins.[23] (In 1960, Vanderbilt was still segregated at the undergraduate level.) He also reported on the trial of another divinity student who was attacked at a sit-in, arrested for "disorderly and offensive conduct," acquitted, and allowed to remain in school.[24] Though most Vanderbilt students were against integration, and only a few faculty members open advocates of it, Blount's reporting reflects no bias. In addition to his newspaper work, he was successful socially and academically; he was initiated into Sigma Chi fraternity and tapped by Phi Eta Sigma, a freshman scholastic honor society for those who had a grade-point average of 2.5 or better on a 3.0 scale during their first semester.[25]

As his sophomore year opened, Blount's range of reporting extended. In a first-person account, he told students about the poetry and the eighteen kinds of coffee available at "The Tulip Is Black," an off-campus coffeehouse "next to the barbershop."[26] His byline appeared in all but two issues (in some, all bylines appeared to be cut for space). He polled students on a perennially favorite topic—the relationship of the sexes at Vanderbilt—and in March 1961 wrote a detailed history of periodically defunct campus humor magazines.[27] Blount was named humor editor of a new literary magazine after citing his aims on the application: "We don't intend to feature iron-lung jokes, bathroom humor, bedroom stuff that is worse (or better) than spicy, or anything smacking seriously of sacrilege (unless, of course, it is at the expense of someone else's religion)." Significantly, *Vagabond* was to be "a student revolution against the 'ethereal type of literature.'"[28]

At the annual literary symposium, Blount reported on a paper by the literary scholar Austin Warren and on a short story reading by Katherine Anne Porter, including her response to a student's (possibly Blount's) question: "Miss Porter pointed out that 'you learn to write, though I hate to say it, by writing. That's one of the dull little truths you might as well settle down with.'"[29] He wrote the story announcing the return of John Crowe Ransom, Fugitive poet, Agrarian, New Critic, alumnus, and former faculty member, who was retiring from Kenyon but would teach the fall semester at Vanderbilt.[30] Demonstrating that he was himself a literary man, Blount wrote about an intramural field once used for intercollegiate football but soon to become the site for a new law school building. The front-page feature, as well-read insiders could see, was sprinkled with allusions to Oliver Wendell Holmes's "Old Ironsides"; to make certain nobody took his righteous indignation seriously, Blount related the removal of the landmark to the critical water shortage for squirrels that the new construction would cause.[31] In the spring semester, Blount was named associate editor of the university orientation handbook; he was also a member of the Interfraternity Council and the Student Christian Association and was chapter editor for Sigma Chi.[32]

After a summer of work at the New York *Morning Telegraph*, a racing paper that offered summer jobs to Grantland Rice scholars, Blount returned in the fall of 1961 to begin his junior year as news editor, serving under Lamar Alexander. Alexander went on to become an aide to Richard Nixon and for two terms was the governor of Tennessee; he is now president of the state university at Knoxville. In his review of Blount's 1989 collection, *Now, Where Were We?*, Alexander remembers telling Blount, on a motorcycle ride to deliver *Hustler* copy to the printer, "*You'll* be *our* James Thurber." Alexander knew older people thought Thurber was the funniest writer in America, and he "was trying to say that Roy would grow up to be the funniest writer of *our* generation. And he has."[33]

With the new title came new opportunities in reporting and a personal column on the editorial page. In the first issue, Blount interviewed Ransom with uncharacteristic reverence. The poet and critic was at Vanderbilt for only one semester "because he must get back to his new home in Ohio, where his large flower gardens must be tended to. In the spring he has to uncover his roses."[34] The news editor also sought to assuage the ancient enmity between Vandy students and Nashville police by riding with two policemen on their night shift and offering a first-person account; a photograph of Blount with two other police officers accompanied his story intended "to improve relations." With the police, Blount saw a stabbing scene and described the victim on an operating table that was "covered with paper because too much blood flows in the emergency room of Hubbard Hospital for sheets to be used. As I watched him being worked on, a grey kitten wandered into the waiting room, stepped on a spot of blood, and shook his paw in disgust."[35]

When the "regenerated" literary magazine finally appeared, after a change in chief editors in February 1962, the *Hustler* reviewer called the commentary by Blount and Anne Evans, based on the *New Yorker* "Talk of the Town" column, not as funny as it would have been had *Vagabond* appeared as scheduled in the fall. More timely and "chuckle-provoking" was Blount's two-page poem about the culinary preferences of the anteater, "Song (and Dance) with Ants."[36]

The campus humorist appeared when Blount created and cultivated as alter ego and foil a character called Sanders, "a short, roundish student who might be described as dumpy," a pipe smoker who is generally grouchy, untidy, and conservative. After Sanders chided Blount for having admitted to being "65% liberal," the columnist reconsidered, recalculated, and confessed to being "60%."[37] (Blount identified himself as a political liberal, but he had opposed adding a majorette for the Vanderbilt band.)[38] In addition to trying out this routine, Blount also demonstrated his wit by examining shoddy writing from the vantage of a higher literary sensibility. The opening paragraph of a column criticizing a local poet manqué, a prominent Nashville newspaperman who was also a member of the Vanderbilt Board of Trust and a former *Hustler* editor, illustrates a prose style remarkable for its economy and edge and introduces a columnist taught to analyze bad poetry after the fashion of Ransom's reading of "Trees": "Any suspicions I might have had that poetry is being neglected in the Athens of the

South were dispelled Monday when I picked up my Nashville Banner and saw that nearly thirty-two column inches of its front page was taken up by a great, rambling colossus of a poem by James G. Stahlman, who besides being Nashville's biggest poet is publisher of the Banner. (Anyone bothered by the metaphor 'rambling colossus' had best look at the poem before he says anything.)"[39]

Further evidence that Blount had not given up on his ambitions to be a humorist appears in a column in which the writer suggested that more should be done to present the college professor "not as a scrawny, thick-lensed introvert, but as a red-blooded, vigorous American man and intrepid leader in the search for truth." Blount moved from a reverie about Vanderbilt professors as stars of contemporary television shows—in academized versions of "Bonanza" and "Have Gun, Will Travel"—to a promotion of a student production of *The Male Animal.* Boosting James Thurber made the columnist "feel like a crippled kid playing charity football for the benefit of the New York Giants." The professor in the play (and, by extension, Thurber) was cited as one of the columnist's "four all-time heroes," together with Holden Caulfield, Robert Benchley, and Audie Murphy.[40]

Although—perhaps because—the humor columns were appearing in the same paper, often on the same page, as Max Shulman's "On Campus" sketches in national advertisements for Marlboro cigarettes, Blount did not imitate the style of Shulman, well known for *The Many Loves of Dobie Gillis.* In fact, even within the Sanders routine Blount found humor in substance, not verbal tricks. Turning the passion of his rhetoric into self-effacement, a habit he would pursue as a mature humorist, Blount sought the detached, ironic view of Holden Caulfield and coupled it with the befuddlement of Benchley, but the persona in its budding stages is that of the literary man, the thinker, the would-be professor. Though his humor often commented on sports, Blount did not appear headed toward a career as the next Grantland Rice.

In the personal columns published during his junior year, Roy Blount (he had yet to use *Jr.* in his byline) was also cultivating the objective editorial voice. On the most important topic of the day, he expressed a rational and, at times, passionate commitment to racial integration. In "Touchy Composition in Black and White," sprinkled with boldfaced paragraphs, he argued, "Integration wouldn't hurt Vanderbilt. The University would affect the Negro students more than they would affect the University. It would cost the University money, of course, but it would be worth the expense."[41] Three months later, he took issue with a Vanderbilt official who said the university would be integrated "when it's time":

That, my friend, is what the cow said two seconds before the tornado. It is always time, and if we had to live cramped like a Negro we would realize that; but when it's really time, Vanderbilt will have to move as sure as fire, and it may have to trot.

Vanderbilt has no authority to decide when it should move, or whom of those who can learn it should teach. Hurry up, please, it's time.[42]

Despite Vanderbilt's high academic reputation, Blount found the campus intellectual climate less than lively. In a column that opened with Emerson's description of the American scholar as "man thinking," Blount concluded, "Vanderbilt will never become the University it should be until its students become men thinking, and liking to think, rather than men answering 'here' to roll call after roll call."[43] At the end of his junior year, after holding his grade point average at 2.6, he was tapped into the Omicron Delta Kappa leadership-honor society and named 1962–63 editor of the *Hustler*.[44] Though obviously a student leader, bearing heavy responsibility during a time of controversy, Blount was never too proud for humor. He closed out the year with a limerick that showed his success in finally finding a rhyme for *Aix*, where the Vanderbilt-in-France program was located:

> A Vanderbilt coed in Aix
> Lost touch with the code that protects.
>   With an unspoken "yes,"
>   She'd so oft acquiesce,
> That soon it became a reflex.[45]

When Blount became *Hustler* editor, most of his opinions on campus and national issues were channeled into the first-person-plural editorials. Though the voice of the newspaper also reflected his own style and wit, the editorials form a counterpoint to the first-person-singular columns and the news features that bear his byline and distinctive style. When former Miss America Maria Beale Fletcher matriculated, it was Blount who interviewed her and reported that "she said she wanted to be alone and let herself go. In an afterthought, she made it clear that she didn't mean she was going to let herself go very far."[46]

Learning the technique of speaking the most offensive opinions through the mouths of others, he wrote a personal column in which he imagined a fraternity rush in which famous people would be assessed and probably cut by typical Vanderbilt Greeks. About Ralph Bunche, Blount had his character say, "The way I see it, the problem is whether this guy will help us enough to justify the expense of installing a separate water fountain."[47] Although the unsigned opinions running under the masthead spoke the opinions of the newspaper, the voice in them was as personal as it was institutional. In an editorial advocating improvement in the notoriously cacophonous Vanderbilt marching band, the *Hustler* said, "The Vanderbilt band has traditionally done as much for the spirit of Vanderbilt students as Jesse James' band did for the spirit of the Missouri Bankers Association."[48]

When he started his year as editor, Blount pledged that the *Hustler* would "take a long look at Southernism, conservatism, the ideal University embodying the best characteristics of these principles, and Vanderbilt as the embodiment of that ideal."[49] The paper lived up to the promise. Editorials called attention to the violence over integration at Ole Miss, and the editor urged the Student Senate to take a stand. When it did not, an editorial charged, "It looks like another big year for the Student Senate. . . . The riots at Ole Miss drew no response from Vanderbilt's version of Capitol Hill. . . . No senator seems to think there is anything much wrong with Vanderbilt that a debate tournament or a convocation or a college bowl match won't fix."[50]

The Senate president returned the volley in the next issue in a long letter suggesting that "the *Hustler*'s seeming unawareness of what the Senate is actually doing can be explained, though not justified, by the editor's absence from all Senate meetings," adding that "the Senate will dream of the days when the front page of the *Hustler* did not contain 10 typographical errors."[51] An editor's note caught the letter writer in a misquote but allowed that he was probably too busy counting typos to get important matters right. In a fifteen-hundred-word, typo-free answer occupying the entire editorial space, the editor formally elevated the tone of the argument, beginning with a headnote from John Milton, "Where there is much desire to learn, there of necessity will be much arguing, much writing, many opinions, for opinion in good men is but knowledge in the making." Patiently, the editorial pointed out that the paper had merely observed in the student senators symptoms of an illness, "lockjaw," and it concluded that a discussion of the Ole Miss riots "might help a few Vanderbilt people think."[52]

In his personal column in the same issue, Blount invoked the Vanderbilt Agrarians, a group of writers that included several of the Fugitive poets, and in particular Donald Davidson, who was still a gray eminence on the campus, to argue that the modern South had done a poor job of preserving its best qualities. In a boldfaced paragraph, Blount wrote, "The South has definitely acted in bad grace in the years since the publication of I'll Take My Stand, but its bad grace hasn't been, by and large, for a good cause. As people will do, Southerners have attempted to hold on to simple conventions without considering the principles behind them." Many modern blacks, he contended, have "all the advanced ambitions and spiritual desires of highly civilized human beings." He made no allusion to Robert Penn Warren's defense of segregation in the Agrarian treatise, but he did attempt to sustain the connection between industrialization and the collapse of the South's society by implying that Southerners fighting integration have no energies left to fend off the "imitation Disneylands and soot-billowing factories." Blount concluded, "If we had remembered the beliefs of the Old South and treated the Negro fairly and according to his intelligence, those who urge integration would have a less telling argument. But we have remembered the wrong things, and soon the South may be just about like the rest of the country only not as integrated yet."[53]

For all its zeal in support of integration and its criticism of Mississippi officials, the *Hustler* took issue with Attorney General Robert Kennedy after he threatened to cut off federal funds if Mississippi did not comply with court rulings. The *Hustler* compared Kennedy to Mississippi's governor, calling him "as misguided and as poor a public servant as Ross Barnett, and more dangerous because he is on the side of sanity." Rising on the updrafts of his own rhetoric, the editorialist said that such activity as Kennedy proposed "will carry this country into decline and fall more surely than creeping socialism, rioting, intolerance, ignorance, or the awesome combination of nepotism and Catholicism."[54] After Blount was personally congratulated by a fellow student for being anti-Catholic, an editorial the following week called attention to "the editor's tendency to make jokes even in the most serious context." Pleading *nostra culpa,* the editorial asked any reader who "divines bigotry or a petty motive" in the newspaper's opinion pieces to "consider giving us the benefit of the doubt, for we may be making a feeble, but well-intentioned attempt at wit."[55]

Blount's emphasis on civil rights in the South attracted letters from Governor Barnett and from Hodding Carter—the Greenville, Mississippi, editor who supported integration—that made national news in an Associated Press story summing up student journalism in the region. [56] Extensive attention to the sit-in controversy in news stories and editorials also prompted a letter from a conservative English professor that criticized the press but redeemed the *Hustler* editor with faint praise: "Now and again, Blount himself can shake free of such grave and pompous arrogance for a reprieve of witty balance. . . . This was a whiff of fresh air in an otherwise suffocating air of preachment and recrimination."[57]

In a personal column commenting on books recently published by two alumni whose work had obviously influenced him, Blount juxtaposed the lives of "strange columnfellows," the conservative Donald Davidson and Ralph McGill, the liberal Atlanta editor and publisher, two men who "could stage a debate that would sum up the last quarter century of ideological conflict in the South." Acknowledging the power of Davidson, Blount trod softly: "The Southern attitude has changed enough so that to many of us young liberalized Southerners Davidson's opinions seem fresher and more stimulating than McGill's, but McGill, thanks to the decay in the South of old values, has the upper hand, and rightly so. The two men are strongly opposed, but both have, in very different ways, exerted strong civilizing influences on the South, and both should mean a good deal to us."[58]

Five years later, when Davidson died and Blount was an editorial columnist for the *Atlanta Journal,* he wrote two columns about his former writing and literature teacher, remembering talking "fairly rewardingly with him a couple of times, over peanut-butter crackers in his office, about writing prose." Blount admired the way Davidson and the other Agrarian writers who produced *I'll Take My Stand* had resisted industrialism, and he compared their attitudes to those of "young radicals who are fighting the impersonality of the military-industrial-labor complex" and of the advocates of black power, for "both were separatist" and "both tried to rally deep-dyed ethnic pride and values against inferiority in the face of blandly assimilating, dehumanizing technocracy." But Blount rejected Davidson's white supremacy and recognized it as a barrier between them: "Since I spent my first two years in college realizing that that kind of spirit was my enemy and the second two years writing editorials against it, and since I didn't know a word of Greek, Mr. Davidson and I didn't have much to say to each other in my formative years." In a follow-up column two days later, Blount acknowledged that Davidson was a man "whole in his acts."[59]

In the *Hustler* columns, Blount's zeal for integration did not push him into sentimentality. Occasionally the Holden Caulfield tone of voice showed through, when his self-consciousness quickened. When Blount visited Fisk University, also in Nashville, to attend a banquet at which fraternity matters were discussed, his black counterpart asked, "Is your daddy Greek?" Though himself the secretary of Sigma Chi, Blount said that the "honest resolution of interracial difficulties" would not be brought about when superficial, not real, problems were examined. "A conversation among white and Negro students about bream-fishing or Kant would have in its small way a salutary effect on racial relations," he said, "but such a conversation about the adminis-tration of the sort of brotherhood (not to disparage it completely) rep-resented by Greek letters tends to be in itself misleading and empty." He worked his way to the statement, "It is so much easier . . . to neither love nor hate."[60]

Roy Blount's student journalism reflects, in sum, the good fortune that results when talent, energy, and opportunity meet. He proved himself a facile writer, able to handle all the assignments of the *Hustler*—though, considering his eventual success in national journal-ism, he never assigned himself a sports story—and to produce volumes of copy. His writing is fluid and authoritative, observant of the forms of news, feature, column, and editorial writing but always transcend-ing the forms. His style was distinctive from the first story he wrote to his final, farewell column, more than twice the usual eight hundred words, a tribute to the place where his personality as a writer was made public. Important stories, national and local, had lifted his journalism above the commonplaces of campus news. The civil rights movement, the retirement of the old chancellor and the selection of the new, and the firing and hiring of the football coach had given him opportunities few college journalists could expect in a four-year span.

Although Blount's wit, range, and command of the language set his newspaper writing apart, he did not advertise his serious academic in-terest in literature. That side of Blount's development is demonstrated in three essays, two critical and one humorous, published in 1962 and 1963 in *Spectrum,* a semiannual magazine "reflecting the Honors Pro-gram and other student writings at Vanderbilt." The two critical es-says, together with a humor sketch three times the length of an average *Hustler* column, revealed a widely read, articulate student of literature who could write cogent, confident, and unstilted literary analysis.

In "Frozen Leopard: Hemingway and the Code," published in September 1962 (which means it was probably written for an English class during his junior year), Blount joined in on the bashing that followed the writer's death the year before. Although he was respectful of Hemingway's prose style and understood why Hemingway had clung to the code, Blount saw the Hemingway hero as one who, like Hamlet, "derives a security from spiritual sterility, death," who "becomes a very good loser," and who "devotes his life to a concrete code and a disciplining ritual that protects him from further disillusionment." Hemingway created a code that enabled him to act with confidence but also "kept him from daring to explore the great and noble questions." Thus, the writer reflected in the fiction "ignores the torture and triumph of fully realized humanity to achieve a shallow victory of order and dignity."[61]

In the spring issue of *Spectrum,* Blount published his first long humorous essay, a twenty-five-hundred-word, Benchleyesque ramble through the writer's uneasiness with telephones, his sister's friends, and horseback riding. He takes no swipes at the Thoroughbred Racing Association, his benefactor through the Grantland Rice scholarship, but he does learn something from his failure to herd properly while astride a five-thousand-dollar bulldogging horse. He awakes the next morning "no satyr but a wiser man."[62] Not only was it apparent from the long essay that he was influenced by Benchley—he had published one column in praise of the man who failed to graduate from Harvard "because he wrote the answer to one of his final exam questions, on the legal difficulties surrounding the Newfoundland fish hatcheries, from the point of view of the fish"—but it was also obvious in the final *Spectrum* essay that Blount had thought long and thoroughly about comedy and humor.[63]

The fruits of that thinking are reflected in an essay on Shaw and comedy, written during Blount's senior year and published the September after he graduated. Blount saw Shaw's comic personae in contrast to Hemingway's "barren and stoic characters"; actions by Shavian heroes, possessing a "characteristically English hardheadedness," generated the humor that averted tragedy. Adopting as an analytical device the polarities of fire and ice, the Apollonian and Dionysian modes useful in describing the relationship between form and passion in the study of tragedy, Blount said the same forces exist in comedy. "From Dante to Dondi, comedy differs from tragedy essentially in that, to the extent that it brings about the enlightenment that can be borne by its characters in the future, it always has a happy ending," he wrote, before shifting the focus to the humor inherent in comedy. He noted Bergson's definition of the laughable as "that which involves the disruption of a certain rigidity" and cited the comment by a character in Castiglione's *Book of the Courtier* who says that "what we laugh at is nearly always something incongruous but not amiss." Blount called the joke "the model and molecule of comedy" because it introduces the conflict between the rigid and the natural, the ice and the fire, yet resolves matters so that "on the whole things are not amiss at all, and we can appreciate the situation with a laugh rather than a wince." He distinguished between Shakespeare's comedy and Shaw's: "Shakespeare's attitude is one that engenders love songs, heartbreak, and babies, but Shaw's is the more sensible and stable." Begging the question of whether the polarities are by necessity mutually exclusive, Blount favored Shaw's comic characters because they possess "common sense" that is both "cool and fluent" and that "dilutes passion and inundates stubborn principle"; moreover, they have a "natural continuity" that is "both objective and warm" and that "makes man's eternal conflicts seem both trivial and part of something eternal."[64]

To place the Shaw essay in the context of Blount's career, with the Vanderbilt years in the background and his publishing career before him, is to see how clearly he had come to realize his aims and his abilities and to have made a conscious choice about the kind of humorist he wanted to be. He had already come down on the side of the cool, commonsensical, dispassionate, and openly manipulative "comedy" and "humor" in Shaw, and he had already established the elements of his own humor. His persona moved across a wide range of subjects, academic, political, and social; he had a politically liberal sensibility, without being doctrinaire; and he had established his own love-hate relationship with the South. The irony in the editorials and straight opinion columns kept him from lapsing into preachment, and the style and perspective in the humor pieces allowed him to approach the trivial and the domestic. True to his later writings, the doggerel was in counterpoint to the rational and conventional, ensuring that the persona would be thought of as wild and irreverent, with serious principles but an unserious attitude toward them. It is obvious from the *Hustler* writings that Blount understood the importance of the persona he was creating, the performer on the page, moving like an athlete, offending and defending, and evading all labels except one.

Blount saw himself, in short, as a literary humorist, and he made plans to be a writer who was also a teacher. His promise as a scholar was recognized at Vanderbilt and, by his senior year, beyond. He was tapped into Phi Beta Kappa and graduated from Vanderbilt in June 1963 with high honors in English; after receiving his second prestigious scholarship—a Woodrow Wilson Fellowship to Harvard—he set out to combine the roles of academician and professional writer. With that image of his future in mind, Roy Blount left the South.

Harvard, the Army, and Home Again

Roy Blount has written little about his year as a graduate student in English at Harvard, but it appears to represent a watershed in his career. Though Vanderbilt University often boasted of being the "Harvard of the South," the Ivy League school did not prove so hospitable. Professors were not as available to students as they had been to Blount at Vanderbilt, where he was not only a brilliant and clubbable student but also the voice of the campus.[65] When graduate school crops up in his humor, it is often associated with strident argument and with arrogant misapprehensions of the South and Southern writing. Whereas his passion for literature had not abated, Blount wrote later that studying it at Harvard was "like learning about women at the Mayo Clinic."[66] Living in Cambridge was not his first experience as an adult residing above the Mason-Dixon line, and it came at the right time for him to explore the persona of the Southerner doomed to (actually *blessed* by) life Up There.

Although his writing during this period apparently was limited to academic papers, Blount stored up the experiences that provide some of the autobiographical asides in *Crackers* and that, coupled with experiences from the years he has lived in the North since 1968, now dominate his humor. Describing a class that he liked, called "Difficult Fiction," he recollected his spluttering defense of Faulkner after an African with an "unnaturally *crisp*" voice had denounced Faulkner for his treatment of "non-Western people." As Blount felt the class consensus turning against one who spoke with a redneck accent but who had supported integration and criticized major college football, he hit on the comic tone that gave him his persona and his appeal to audiences North and South.

I *liked* this class. I liked Mr. Monroe Engel, who taught it, though he hadn't had much to say to me since he'd found out that I was going into the Army the following year. I liked not only *Absalom, Absalom!* but also *What Maisie*

Knew and *The Good Soldier* and *Under the Volcano* and other books we read. All my life I had wanted to be somewhere where people argued about books. (At Vanderbilt, where I had just spent four years, we had had grotesque race-relations arguments, punctuated by well-read coeds' savage cries of "Would you want to take a *shower* with them?") And now that I had reached such a place, I found myself dismissed as a person with an incriminating accent. "Well, just kiss my ass, all of you all," I thought partly, but only *partly*.[67]

Not one to lose his humor, especially by attempting to win the sectional argument, Blount described in the essay his eventual friendship with the African student who was critical of Faulkner, and he returned his persona to the referential center of the debate. It is true that, as an ROTC cadet at Vanderbilt, he had a commission as a second lieutenant, but he had already made up his mind that he would not continue for a Ph.D. degree in English, at Harvard or elsewhere. Blount performed well in his classes and completed his master's degree within an academic year (no thesis was required); however, he apparently had discovered that for him literary humor and literary scholarship were not compatible, and he found that narrow, academic publishing would not be as satisfying as writing for a broader, well-educated readership.

In 1964, at the conclusion of his year at Harvard, he married Ellen Pearson, a Waxahachie, Texas, English major he had met at Vanderbilt, and he entered the army. Though the Vietnam conflict was escalating and was, at last, being called a war, Blount was assigned to desk work in the quartermaster's corps and fulfilled his two-year obligation at bases in New York State. During that time, he wrote for *Atlanta Magazine* (his father was *not* board chairman then) one article about "an all-time, all-star, Georgia-native baseball team" that, he recalls, "the editors rewrote outrageously without consulting me and published without a by-line." He also went back to humor. He sent the *New Yorker* a humorous sketch about an owl and received "a nice long letter from an editor named Hemenway, saying that he'd wanted to buy it but the final decision had gone against it." Blount continued to send new pieces to the magazine and to rewrite the owl sketch, and the notes of rejection "kept getting shorter and shorter." By the time he was hired by the *Atlanta Journal* in 1966, he had "stopped sending humorous pieces to national magazines."[68]

A referral from a college friend, Kim Chapin, brought Blount back to Georgia. Chapin, a sportswriter for the *Journal,* had been a Grantland Rice scholar a year behind Blount and news editor of the *Hustler* under Blount. (Blount once followed Chapin out of an airplane on a parachute jump, which became the topic for a *Hustler* column; Blount followed Chapin again in 1968 when he left the *Journal* to join Chapin as a writer for *Sports Illustrated*. In his review of *Crackers* twelve years later, Chapin drew on an awareness from undergraduate days that "Roy Blount views life through a different prism.")[69] Blount worked at the *Journal* from 24 October 1966, shortly after he was honorably discharged as a first lieutenant, to 12 July 1968. He hired on as a reporter but had not lost his eye for the humorous opening. To the question on the Atlanta newspaper's job application form asking, "Have you ever been arrested?" Blount answered, "No." To the inquiry as to why, he responded, "Luck and clean living."[70] He and Ellen moved to Atlanta with their newborn daughter, Ennis, and he began to experience the life of the newspaper journalist in the South.

Beginning as a $110-a-week staff member, handling obits and rewrites from the morning paper, he missed his first deadline, a rewrite from the morning *Constitution* about a "paregoric-crazed gunman." Blount's talents were quickly recognized by the *Journal* editors. He was promoted to general assignment reporter and covered Cobb County, another part of metropolitan Atlanta. He reported on fires, murder trials, and a speech by Stokely Carmichael, the black activist, but backed away from the chance to expose a politician, because "the man had paid the money back and he was said to have terrible family problems."[71] On the side Blount wrote for the *New York Times*; among the stories, which ran without bylines, was an interview with Martin Luther King, Jr., about the Poor People's Campaign. His weekly pay was raised $15 in January 1967, and he moved to the editorial department in March, with another $10-a-week raise.[72] His responsibilities included editorial writing, editorial and op-ed page makeup, and, best of all, a personal column, which was running three times a week by the time he left the paper.

The editorial page was directed by Jack Spalding, who was listed on the *Journal* masthead as editor though he did not oversee news coverage. The editorial page of the *Journal* was considered less liberal than that of its sister paper, the *Constitution,* which bore the stamp of two of the South's leading civil rights advocates, the publisher, Ralph McGill, and the editor, Eugene Patterson; however, according to Reese Cleghorn, the associate editor (now dean of the College of Journalism at the University of Maryland), the *Journal,* during the time he and

Blount were associated, became the first to oppose the war in Vietnam and was no less liberal in its stand for racial justice. Spalding gave the editorial writers maximum leeway in selecting topics, although the editorial page generally reflected the editor's instincts.[73] When writers disagreed with the newspaper's position, they were allowed to express their opinions in personal columns. (Cleghorn differed by personally endorsing Maynard Jackson, who was running against Herman Talmadge for the U.S. Senate and who eventually became Atlanta's first black mayor.) Because the editorial staff of the afternoon paper had to meet a 9 A.M. deadline, Spalding usually conducted a short editorial staff meeting in which topics were assigned. None of the writers specialized, and Blount joined the others in writing about all topics. The editorials were usually written and "circularized" within an hour of the staff meeting.

Most often topical and political, as his *Hustler* columns had been, though less literary, the *Journal* pieces gave Blount a chance to cultivate a style more journalistic than academic and to return to humor. Recruited as "young blood" for the editorial page, Blount had a perspective and style that set him apart. "He wrote with panache," Cleghorn said. "He invaded the pages."

The perspective Blount had developed at Vanderbilt stood him in good stead in Atlanta. Never one to shy away from the hottest controversies, he generally cooled them down, as a Shaw character might, by withholding enthusiasm and retreating into the subjective for a fresher point of view. The persona (because of his father's prominence he had added the *Jr.*) in the Blount *Journal* columns enters polemical arguments reluctantly, if at all, and would rather be dealing with subjects less charged and more amusing.

One topic not to be avoided was the Vietnam War. In the second column, published in June 1967, Blount made his most direct attack on the war; he established a literary-historical context, relating the Vietnam War to the Mexican War and himself to Thoreau: "I am convinced that our present war, though not so selfishly motivated as the Mexican (which gave us California), is uncalled for, misdirected, futile, and damaging to everyone involved." Yet, unlike Thoreau, Blount had been civilly obedient and had served his time in the army because of a "many-sided reluctance to go to prison."[74] Thereafter, his criticisms of the war were, for the most part, glancing shots.

In fact, by December 1967 Blount seemed weary of the news event that was providing the lead story in almost every issue of the *Journal*.

In "Ours Is Just to Reason Why," an allusion to Tennyson that he, as layout editor, probably put in the headline, he recalled his years as a begrudging ROTC cadet at Vanderbilt and his two years in the army as "a melancholy bureaucrat compelled to go about dressed as a man of war." But he was less frontal in his assault and, with subtle rhetoric, related the war to racism: "I don't suppose I should quibble over the reasons why people are willing to go fight my country's battles; but then again, maybe I should. War today, from what I can tell, is for America an aridly specialized and localized pursuit, conducted by men like Gen. Westmoreland, whose contribution to race-relations a while back was to commend the Army's Negroes for being 'proficient in a cross-section of technical skills.' Unfortunately, whole, nonprofessional men are put to use by it."[75]

However strongly Blount might have supported racial justice, he appeared instinctively to know when cant threatened and how to counter it with frank humor. For instance, in "You Wouldn't Say 'Nigroo Power,'" Blount remembered his senior year at Vanderbilt, when students had voted two to one against integration, though the trustees had approved it, and he sprang from that memory to the question of "the term one should use to designate Negroes." Positioning himself, again, as a liberal, he found a way to write—while condemning, of course—*darky, gentleman of color, chocolate,* and *nigra.* Blount said he would prefer to be called *black,* if he were black; but, as a white man, he lacked the authority to offer a dogmatic solution: "I suppose a good deal of all this is none of my business." To indicate that he was not leaving the matter on such abstract terms, Blount ended the column by wishing he were at an Atlanta restaurant when Vernon Jordan entered and was greeted by a white writer with the shout, "Vernon, it's wonderful to see a great big black face in here."[76]

Many of the eight-hundred-word *Journal* columns contain ideas Blount reworked in later essays. One favorite of reviewers, "The Socks Problem," published in 1982 in *One Fell Soup,* appeared first as "Whatever Happened to Socks?" on 12 July 1967. To compare the original with the expanded revision is to see how Blount has responded to changing times and readers. Absent from the later version is any mention of the wife that washes socks; instead Blount switches to "his or her" references with respect to socks, sex, and the sex of socks. The readership of a national publication appearing fifteen years after the *Journal* column would respond to the addition of sly sexual allusions— to the single shrunken sock "that may require lubrication" and to socks that separate because socks "don't mate for life." But retained in the 1982 essay (with *devil* capitalized and *papers* changed to *media*) is the 1967 basic insight into where lost socks go:

> Let us assume, then, in the absence of any compelling evidence to the contrary, that socks die and are reincarnated, perhaps in groups, as a variety of garments.
>
> It is the work of the devil—maybe—or maybe the sock-and-rummage sale cabal, which the papers never tell you anything about.[77]

Drawing on Vanderbilt and army experiences, contemporary Atlanta, state politics (he had the good fortune to be writing when Lester Maddox was governor), and national events, Blount's columns were devoted to making humor, not opinions. Given loose rein by Spalding, he sought out the incongruous and even found a way to insert his poetry. His limericks about Georgia towns with human names appeared first in *Journal* columns that were reworked and published in *Atlanta Magazine* and, eventually, in *Crackers,* to wit:

> A lonesome old soul of McRae
> Sat home saying, "There ain't no wae."
>   Till a lady from Bimini
>   Slid down his chimini
> And he granted, "Oh, well, there mae."[78]

While he was in Atlanta, Blount had one more chance to see whether he wanted to be a college professor. In the fall quarter of 1967 and the spring quarter of 1968, he taught a freshman composition night course at Georgia State University, an experience about which he has not written. He needed the money—$400 a quarter—and he wanted to find a place to talk about literature. He found it difficult to get the students to write about what they actually did; they tended to abstract, even when attempting to describe their jobs. For one assignment, Blount came into the classroom wearing a funny hat and juggling two tennis balls and an orange. "I walked around oddly for two or three minutes," he said, "and then asked the students to write about what they had seen." Some still abstracted ("the instructor walked around acting crazy") but others did well. Another stratagem was more effective: after the class had read *Nineteen Eighty-Four,* Blount asked the students to imagine they had been captured by the totalitarian government and had been given three minutes to prove that democratic freedoms were valid. Although he liked teaching, he saw how grading papers would siphon off the energy he needed for writing. "I found myself writing essays in the margins," he said, and realized that "students were not my best audience."[79]

Although he had been at the newspaper for less than two years, by 1968 Blount had, according to Cleghorn, "done about what he could do." The *Journal* editors had seen that there was "nothing ordinary about his writing or the way his mind worked," and Cleghorn remembered thinking that "this guy was on his way to being the leading humorist of the country."[80] Blount had fulfilled an apprenticeship in editorial and humor writing for the broadest and probably the most severe general audience, which, to judge from the dearth of letters to the editor responding to either mode of his writing, did not appreciate him as much as his editors did. Although his diffident, slantwise approach and his selection of domestic topics kept him from being pigeonholed as an editorial enfant terrible, his mention of racial matters teased out the more hard-core bigots, and he had the satisfaction of liberal editorial writers in the South of the late 1960s who felt their writing hit home. In *Crackers* he recalled his pride at receiving a telegram that read: "COONLOVER [RALPH] MCGILL, COONLOVER [GENE] PATTERSON, COONLOVER [REESE] CLEGHORN, NOW COONLOVER BLOUNT. HELL WILL BURN YOUR TRAITOR SOULS"(52). Blount was ready to leave the South, but not because he was afraid of the response to his opinions. In one essay in *Crackers,* he said, "For a while it was good, writing for a newspaper in Atlanta; you could achieve a measure of significance just by standing opposed to the forces of hate. . . . But the truth was, Southern liberalism had about been mapped out and settled. And yet, people would occasionally take their money out of my daddy's savings and loan because of things I'd written" (21). In another *Crackers* essay, he listed a second reason for leaving the *Journal*: "I wanted to go to New York. Writing for a Georgia outlet is like putting on skits for your parents: you can only go so far. I would sit there at my desk and pound out things which, though I knew they were insufficient to the historical moment, I knew would elicit hysterical phone calls anyway" (23).[81]

The *Sports Illustrated* Years: 1968–75

When Kim Chapin told Roy Blount that *Sports Illustrated* was looking for writers "they could hire cheap," Blount, who was making $150 a week, was ready to go. Although he had never been a sportswriter and had written only three magazine articles, he had included sports topics in his *Journal* column, and he had the 1961 summer experience at the New York racing paper. He was hired in July 1968 as a staff writer at a yearly salary of $11,500, a pay increase of $70 a week. Ellen, who was pregnant with their son John, had a small income from Waxahachie city bonds, and they were able to sell the house they had bought in Atlanta for a $5,000 profit. In New York, they rented a three-bedroom apartment in Greenwich Village for $335 a month. "That was the kind of economy I could understand," Blount said, "unlike the 80s."[82] For more than a year after he left Atlanta, the *Journal* paid him $25 for occasional columns.

Blount's first byline in *Sports Illustrated* appeared over a story about tennis player Clark Graebner on 5 August 1968.[83] His name was published on the masthead the following week in an impressive roster of regular staff and contributing writers, among them Tex Maule, Frank Deford, Dan Jenkins, George Plimpton, and one about whom Blount would himself write later, Myron Cope, a popular sports editor in the hometown of the Pittsburgh Steelers.

It was not long before Blount—who identifies himself as "one of the original subscribers of *Sports Illustrated*"—had found his niche at the magazine. Although his knowledge of sports was slight and his was "a highly underdeveloped bent for punchy athletico-newsmag style," he was soon writing the "Scorecard" roundup column.[84] That assignment allowed Blount to stay in New York City until John Kirven was born in December and for a few months afterward; as soon as baseball spring training started, he was sent south. By that time, he had apparently caught on to the *Sports Illustrated* style, or his own version of it. In a two-thousand-word interview with Johnny Bench, who was twenty-one and starting his second season with the Cincinnati Reds, Blount wrote with acumen and confidence: "For a catcher to rise up amidst his grotesque impedimenta as Bench does, cock his arm like a flash and shoot a ball out with enough velocity to beat a runner to second without either attaining appreciable loft or tailing off at the end is one of the wonders of cultivated nature. The only comparable thing would be a bear that really danced well."[85] Noting that Bench was learning to do some trendy dancing, Blount prophesied that the catcher "would be around long enough for everybody to forget the Funky Broadway. Whatever the dance is 10 to 15 years from now, ballplayers will probably be doing it to Johnny Bench's tune."[86]

Over his seven years as a regular staff writer, Blount averaged better than one long article a month, on a wide range of subjects. His writing, like Bench's throwing, was never lofty and never low. He interviewed and described Willie Mays (saving Mays's rebuff for a comment in *About Three Bricks Shy of a Load*), coauthored long articles with Frank Robinson and Wilt Chamberlain (reserving a Chamberlain episode for a long sketch in "Roy Blount's Happy Hour and a Half"), and overcame one major obstacle inherent in the *Sports Illustrated* style: he learned to imply himself without the liberty of the first person singular—and he learned it early. Coming back to Atlanta in August of 1969, after having been away for a year, he was putatively on assignment to cover the Atlanta Falcons and "to wonder if the South's first .500-or-over professional football team were slouching toward Georgia to be born." But he was also interested in Atlanta and in his own relationship to the city: "In the 1950s and early 60s the city of Atlanta must have been in a state of grace. Somehow it seemed to be urban and yet not hung up. While other cities in the region were stagnating and putting their best police dogs forward, Atlanta won a reputation for progressiveness, efficiency, moderation and even gentility in race relations and municipal affairs."[87] The persona of the writer is thinly veiled by the third-person voice: "An Atlanta boy who listened on the radio to Tech coming from behind again and again by some quirk of fate or character to beat a favored and heavier opponent was likely to become confirmed in a particular sort of white Southern American dream."[88]

The style of *Sports Illustrated* suited the editorialist and the essayist in Blount. Although the stories were not overtly opinion pieces, they were as much interpretative as they were expository. Pressed to do better than television in the way of commentary, writers were freed to write long, insightful essays, using the same literary devices Blount had learned before New Journalism came into vogue. Given a chance to use every technique of prose fiction except first-person narration (and even Blount slipped into that in his last years at *Sports Illustrated*) and given enough space to stretch out a subject, the writers nevertheless had to hold to the body of fact. Whereas they were providing commentary or "color"—and were given such liberties with connotative language that opinion was rarely in doubt—they were also obligated to inform. In sum, the writers were not granted the full indulgences of the fiction writer, the New Journalist, or the humorist. The ethos of the magazine ruled the persona of the writer.

Eventually the camaraderie of the magazine suited Blount, too, as he remembered the *Sports Illustrated* days after having been away for fifteen years:

It took me several years to get into the swing of the place, because I went home to Brooklyn every night instead of hanging out in bars, but after my first marriage broke up I did get into the swing of it, had great times with Dan Jenkins and Bud Shrake and Walter Iooss (photographer) and Sarah Ballard and Ron Fimrite and Stephanie Salter and many others. Pete Axthelm of *Newsweek,* Roger Angell of the *New Yorker,* Jon Walsh and Pete Bonventre of *Inside Sports.* Jack Whitaker of CBS. At Superbowls and back at the office. Lots of staying up half the night telling stories. No supervision, no meetings, just get your story in on time. Seldom had to be at the office, and when you were there, someone was playing catch in the hall or running from office to office in a gorilla suit. A great job for a young man. I work a lot harder now, drink a lot less, don't smoke dope at all, get a lot more sleep, eat a lot healthier, and feel less lively.[89]

The dual obligations of journalist and stylist, of recorder and interpreter, provided a bracket into which Blount fit perfectly, even though he chafed under some of the editing.[90] His ability to write ideal *Sports Illustrated* prose is reflected in many of the profiles, particularly an early article on Billy Martin, who was managing the Minnesota Twins for the second time. Although Martin had described himself as "an organization man," Blount called that assessment an "oversimplification," writing:

During the period referred to he has punched not the organization's clock but one of its vice presidents. He has also come up with the idea for Nun's Day, played Pygmalion to a one-shot Most Valuable Player, masterminded so many thieveries of home that in half a year one of his thieves tied the record, expressed public reservations about Ted Williams, won Joe Frazier's endorsement as the only man in the majors who knows how to handle his fists, threatened to drown Joe Gordon, put up a tomato crop in cans and set fire to the Denver Bears once and the Twins, themselves, twice. Billy the Kid, in short, has not become some faceless, plastic cog.[91]

As a way to circumscribe, literally, the "athletico-newsmag style," to assert his own identity, and to escape the conventional sports beats, Blount sought out odd and offbeat stories. By 1972, he had become so successful that his story about coon hunting ran five thousand words during the hottest part of college and professional football season. As a neutral observer he sided with both the predator and the prey, allowing that although the "raccoon is not the farmer's friend" and that "five or six dogs tearing into a coon in the glow of their owners' hunting light in the night woods do make a glorious tangle of color—redbone, bluetick, black and tan, and various brindles such as English and Plott," nevertheless "the killing of a coon by dogs is one of the ugliest, not to mention least equitable, sporting scenes." Sensing the pleasure of the sport for men and dogs, Blount wrote lyrically, without overwriting, stepping aside to let his subjects deliver the humor:

That is something: to catch the exact drift of a dog way off in the distance, maybe two or three miles, in the dark, in wild country, following its instincts and training through thick cover, running as hard as it can. A good many men go coon hunting three or four or five nights a week, sometimes all night long, in good weather and bad, year round. "In 1964, me and my wife got into it about coon hunting," says John L. Smith of Garland, Texas, a drywall contractor and father of four. "She got mad and said, 'All right, you just go and hunt then!' 'Well, that's good,' I said. I hunted 42 nights in a row, and she never said anything more about it.'"[92]

The end of the story provides a literary answer to the question of which party is right—man, dog, or coon: all three appear as part of a figurative continuum.

The selection of topics indicates that Blount was still thinking like a humorist. In 1973, he interviewed the "world's oldest lifeguard," an eighty-one-year-old man on Cape Cod, and told the story of his life as a retired high school Latin teacher with several intriguing health problems and a brusque attitude toward good swimmers who merely thought they were drowning.[93] That same year, Blount wrote about Jerry Clower, the Southern comedian, who had been a football player at Mississippi State and who had become a popular speaker at sports banquets. In a profile of sixty-five hundred words (long by *Sports Illustrated* standards), the third-person writer addressing a national readership was obviously moved by Clower's humor and by his ability to be Southern without being racist and Bible Belt Christian without being self-righteous: "Clower may be one of the few current-day Christians whose prayers the Lord looks forward to, if they are anything at all like the rest of his conversation, and if such odd elements as punting statistics keep turning up in them. But anybody looking to brand Clower as a regionalist or a redneck might accuse him of espousing conventional pieties. Each of his albums includes an entirely unhumorous sermon on Americanism and decency, and he never says anything bad about sports."[94] Blount described Clower as "a 270-pound, 46-year-old, anti-likker, anti-bigotry, deepwater Baptist Mississippi fertilizer salesman" who "pooches his lips out, waves his arms, imitates a chain saw cutting through a screen door" and can go "'ba-ooo' deep down in his throat like a coon dog."[95]

Although many of the topics, such as Southeastern Conference football, coon hunting, and Clower, sent Blount to the South, he rarely lapsed into Southern idioms. The interlocutor-narrator in his stories speaks a general American, nonregional, *Sports Illustrated* English. The anecdotes and idioms that would later be claimed by Blount's style were left in the dialogue of the characters. The long feature articles do not suggest any ennui, any problems with editors, or the "real strain" Blount says he felt himself under until his last year or two there; in fact, he appeared to have the pattern of description and anecdote down pat.[96] He had perfected the knack of getting close to famous athletes, for finding new angles—often humorous anecdotes—for stories on their personal lives, and for providing readers with a perspective on the context of sports that television could not or would not provide. Yet for Blount, still listed as a "staff writer" in 1973, there appeared to be no other worlds to conquer at *Sports Illustrated.* Once in a profile he had quoted E. B. White's advice to Thurber when Thurber was trying to refine his cartooning style: "If you ever got good, you'd be mediocre."[97] As a sportswriter toiling in the medium of the man he did not expect to follow when he entered Vanderbilt, Blount was never mediocre, but he was as good as he could be.

Looking to the day when he could quit *Sports Illustrated* and freelance, and aware that staffers were forbidden to write about sports for other magazines, Blount had started to play the field early. In the *New York Times Magazine,* he placed a five-thousand-word article about basketball star Pistol Pete Maravich in 1970 and another about Roberto Clemente in April 1972, nine months before the Pirates' star outfielder was killed in a plane crash.[98] Because of the rule forbidding sports freelancing, both articles were published under pseudonyms—the Maravich piece under Noah Sanders (the name of Blount's foil from *Hustler* days, drawn from Winnie-the-Pooh's friend) and the Clemente one under C. R. Ways, the name of a Decatur neighbor's cat.[99] The articles are factual, drawing on the context of basketball and baseball, and are addressed to general readers rather than sports fans. They are also blander than the *Sports Illustrated* writings, with little to betray Blount as the author. Noah Sanders is identified as one "who occasionally plays basketball by himself, imagining whatever other players are necessary," and C. R. Ways is described merely as "a long-time student of baseball." Blount also worked on a piece about a racially troubled New York high school that the *Times* magazine editors didn't print.[100] He finally sold something to the *New Yorker* in 1974, a poem entitled "For the Record," published over his own name and based on a *Newsweek* story about an English ballet dancer named Sleep who outdid Nijinsky by becoming the first person to cross and uncross his legs five times in a single leap. Blount's poem, a mishmash of cadences and echoes of Shakespeare, Wordsworth, Keats, and Ernest Thayer's "Casey at the Bat," with macaronic rhymes, imagines Nijinsky rising again to reclaim the record. Republished as the final item in *One Fell Soup,* the poem ends:

> And now he's really going good.
> Nijinsky, folks, has just *vingt-deux'd.*
> We sense he could on to *cent-deux*
> But evidently doesn't want to.
> For now, with one great closing spring,
> He goes through untold scissoring
> And disappears—a quantum leap—
> And leaves the blinking world to Sleep.[101]

In 1973, the editors gave Blount the assignment that would eventually spring him to do free-lance work, the season of living with the Pittsburgh Steelers that resulted in *About Three Bricks Shy of a Load.* In October 1974, he was also promoted to associate editor, still below the rank of senior writers Deford and Jenkins; he quit the regular staff position in July 1975, and his status was changed to "special contributor." He left on friendly terms and continued—still continues—to write for *Sports Illustrated,* "with much more respectful editing than when I was on the staff."[102] His six-thousand-word essay on possum showing in Alabama, first published in July 1976 and redressed for *Crackers,* testifies to how far he had come since the Johnny Bench interview and how much liberty he was given as a writer who had earned the rights of first-person status. (The title, applied to the possum, fits the writer as well—"His Time Has Come.").

In 1988, Blount summarized his career at the magazine in a third-person autobiographical sketch in the *Playbill* for "Roy Blount's Happy Hour and a Half": "For *Sports Illustrated,* where he was a staff writer and associate editor from 1968 to 1975, he has rafted down the Amazon (attacked by piranha), played baseball with the 1969 Chicago Cubs (hit a ball 350 feet), become (all but athletically) a virtual member of the dynasty years Pittsburgh Steelers, and hung out with Wilt Chamberlain, Yogi Berra, Reggie Jackson and the world's oldest then-living lifeguard."[103] Blount also sees the years with *Sports Illustrated* as more than an opportunity for "good times and great trips": "I have had younger magazine journalists tell me that the *Sports Illustrated* style, which we might describe incompletely as Timestyle infused with personal Texas, was a real influence on American prose. I don't know about that, and I was always wary of lapsing thoroughly into it, but I believe working in its third-person keep-it-hopping context was good for my chops. The job also got me into fancy hotels and people's mamas' houses all over the country and taught me that if you have to write five thousand words in a night, you can."[104]

In more than hundred articles for the magazine, Roy Blount had covered American sports—major, minor, and arguable—succeeding, as his friend Kim Chapin has noted, in viewing "life through a different prism." After the appearance of the first chapters of *About Three Bricks* in July and August of 1974, the direction of Blount's career was fixed. He had succeeded in developing a reputation as a writer with his own latitude and perspective, capable of writing more than sports, and he was ready to step clear of the constraints of regular staff writing. Divorced in 1972, he moved in 1975 to Mill River, in the mountains of western Massachusetts, where his former wife lived and where both could help in the raising of their children. Though he would continue to write excellent expository prose, he set out to make his fortune as the humorist he wanted to be. At thirty-four, he was about to begin trading on his own name, the persona he had created and confirmed.

Chapter Three
The Free-lance Franchise

Free-lance writing is one of the few fields in which you don't get paid . . . if you don't give satisfaction, and you don't get paid much (generally speaking) if you do. How many other American livelihoods depend on sheer productivity?
—Roy Blount, Jr., letter to author, 20 May 1989

No man but a blockhead ever wrote except for money.
—Samuel Johnson, quoted in Boswell's *Life of Johnson*

For Roy Blount the cultivation of the persona of literary humorist has been a practical and concrete experience, a review of which reveals much about the life of a working writer. In 1975, when he gave up a *Sports Illustrated* salary of $26,000 a year to fulfill his dream of becoming an independent writer and humorist, he was divorced, the father of two children, then nine and seven. Restive as a staff writer, he had carefully weighed his prospects and knew that making it alone would be chancy. The author of one widely and favorably reviewed book, *About Three Bricks Shy of a Load,* he had already demonstrated his talent for expository and humorous writing, and he left the magazine with a contributing-writer contract. Soon, however, he learned the price of independence:

For the first twelve months of my free-lance career, July 75–July 76, I grossed $20,000 with no benefits. I had a $12,000 contract with *SI* as a special contributor, which meant that I got $1,000 every month against what I wrote at a rate of $2,000 for a "bonus piece" and on down. This I realize now was pretty poor pay, even at 1975 dollars. I think I wrote a few thousand dollars worth more than that during the first year, and I wrote a *Time* cover story about baseball (a horrible experience) for $2,000 and for $2,500 I did a TV commercial in Pittsburgh for Iron City beer. (Now I turn down offers to do commercials, because I think they would be a betrayal of my franchise, but I liked Iron City beer and I needed the money.)[1]

Despite the drop in income, Blount was "modestly solvent—enough so to put down $17,000 on a $47,000 house." He had about $8,000 in profit-sharing money from the magazine, he had saved most of the $15,000 from *About Three Bricks Shy of a Load,* and he had inherited $30,000 when his father died in 1974. His children were living in Monterey, in western Massachusetts, with their mother and with him when he was at his separate residence in the nearby village of Mill River; Ennis attended public schools through the eighth grade and John through the sixth. In 1976, Blount married Joan Ackermann, whom he had met at Little, Brown, where she was an editor's assistant, on the day in 1974 that he submitted the final draft of *About Three Bricks Shy of a Load.* She also became a free-lance journalist and, later, a playwright, publishing under the name Joan Ackermann-Blount, which she retained after they were divorced in 1989.

The first bit of advice Blount gives to prospective free-lancers is "Don't quit your day job" and the second is "Keep your nut [living expenses] low." In 1975, his Mill River mortgage was $280, and his New York pied-à-terre rented for $235 a month. Still, he felt the "desperation" of the free-lance writer, which he calls "the mother of inspiration":

I never knew what I was going to make in any given year, or month; I never knew how much time a given assignment was going to take me; publications and publishers tend to send checks belatedly; free lance writers are among the few workers who get paid only if their work satisfies; and I have never had any capacity for budgeting. What I do have is a sense of how to satisfy a publication's agenda as well as my own, and a high toleration for jumble, and a knack for judging how long past deadline is actually late. Juggling is important. Once I counted up 28 projects I had going, of which nine were overdue, of which five I hadn't hit a lick on yet. When I say I'm a free lance writer people often say, "You must have a lot of discipline," but that is not the case. Most of my working hours are spent hopping up and down, begrudging the non-conduciveness of loved ones and machinery, glaring disgustedly at what I have written so far, trying to sneak up on my subconscious, and fiddling with unremunerative things.

Blount resented much of the editing of his copy at *Sports Illustrated* and generally finds book editing more congenial to his style. He calls the experience of writing the cover story on baseball for *Time,* the mother magazine of *Sports Illustrated,* "miserable" because the editors wanted "prose to order."[2] At *Sports Illustrated,* however, Blount had the good fortune to run into Gil Rogin, who had published short stories in the *New Yorker* and who moved from staff writer to editor about the time Blount went to the magazine. Rogin assigned those offbeat stories, such as the "oldest living lifeguard," to Blount and protected his copy. The editor's wife at the time, Ruth Rogin, a secretary at the *New Yorker*, "hand carried" Blount's poem "For the Record" into the office of Howard Moss, the poetry editor, and Moss accepted it.[3]

Blount has been successful enough at free lancing to establish other contractual relationships with magazines and to fence with editors. In 1977, when Lee Eisenberg and Geoffrey Norman at *Esquire* offered Blount a sports column, at $1,000 plus $500 expenses monthly, the *Sports Illustrated* editors asked him to choose either a renewed *Sports Illustrated* contract or the *Esquire* column. Blount took the column, which he called "a much less formal and more personal pulpit," in order to return to writing "more or less like myself periodically," as he had done for the *Vanderbilt Hustler* and the *Atlanta Journal*. At *Esquire*, he was allowed to write about subjects other than sports, a fact that attracted the attention of other magazines. Although the *New Yorker* rejected some pieces on what Blount considers "quirky grounds," the magazine began to accept occasional humor pieces, among the first "Whose Who?," a brilliant, fast-forward history of humankind by "a people-item journalist" that is reprinted in *One Fell Soup*.[4] Blount's editor at the *New Yorker* was Roger Angell, author of several sports books, including *The Summer Game*, and the son of Katharine Angell (Mrs. E. B.) White.

At *Esquire*, Blount found another sympathetic editor, Gordon Lish. In 1976, Blount had a contract and $10,000 of a $20,000 advance (with the remainder to come on acceptance of the manuscript) with the Little, Brown publishing company for a book on country music that evolved into *Crackers*. When the manuscript was submitted to Little, Brown in 1979, Blount was told it could not be published before the 1980 presidential election. His agent sent the manuscript to Lish, then an editor at Knopf, who pushed the book through, although Knopf paid only $15,000. "All I had to look at after four years of wrestling with that project was $4,500," Blount said.

Blount believes that *Crackers* would not have been as good a book without Lish's editing. Lish combed the manuscript, word for word, and debated Blount about sentence structure, organization, and punctuation. "We argued about whether there should be a comma between Blount and Jr., things like that," Blount said. "He even accused me of punctuating like an Englishman." But most of all, Lish gave Blount confidence in his skills as a writer and a humorist. "I was glad to have someone go through and tell me where it was boring because it was *all* boring to me by the time I turned it in," Blount said. "I appreciated what [Lish] did because you're very vulnerable when you write a book and someone could have come along and told me it was terrible, and I would have said, 'Yeah, you're right.'" Lish suggested cuts; he told Blount that he was trying too hard to make *Crackers* into a tight, conventional book and that he should include a piece from *Esquire* that did not fit neatly into the whole but was funny. "I was glad because I always feel I should write some kind of proper book, one that makes sense, but he said, 'Nah, go ahead and be crazy.'"[5] (The essay Lish suggested for inclusion is "Things in the Wrong Hands," about a woman who gets glued to a dry cleaner's conveyor.)

Blount was a contributing editor and sports columnist for *Esquire* from 1976 until 1982, when he became a contributing editor for the *Atlantic.* One of the reasons he gives for leaving *Esquire,* in addition to a change in editors that "curdled" a good working relationship, is that he was rankled that *Esquire* editors asked him to rewrite the last lines of paragraphs so that the last line would extend more than halfway across the column and the final line was flush with the right margin. Blount refused to go along with the art editors' requests. The incident was reported in the *Columbia Journalism Review,* and the *Pittsburgh Press-Gazette* ran an editorial applauding Blount, whom it quoted as saying, "I found it impossible to say exactly what I meant and also to fulfill requirements like that."[6] Blount continued as a sometime writer of nonreview articles for *Esquire,* and he was also selling regularly to *Playboy* and *Parade.* When the editorial attitude of *Parade* and *Vanity Fair* toward the Reagan administration became too obsequious to suit Blount, he lost interest in writing for those magazines. "I've never had to feel beholden to any one publication," he said. "They've gotten jealous of one another, but I can live with that. Magazines aren't going to be faithful to me any longer than I can produce what they want; and, as long as I can get away with it, I'm not going to be faithful to what they want me to do unless it's what I want to do."

In 1978, before the relationship with *Esquire* soured, Blount had a chance to return to *Sports Illustrated.* Rogin tried to negotiate a deal that would have brought him back to the magazine staff to write six long pieces a year for $30,000 and left him free to write nonsports pieces for other magazines as well. "I was feeling so insecure financially that I almost went for it," Blount said, "but the *SI* managing editor then, Roy Terrell, started talking to me about loyalty to *SI* and I realized that I would be getting back into the same conflict-of-interest murk that made free-lancing so problematical when I was on the staff before."

Going to the *Atlantic,* as it turned out, was a "great break." The editor, Bill Whitworth, proved more "consistently receptive" to his humor pieces than the *New Yorker* was. Thanks to an increase in the editorial budget by publisher Mort Zuckermann, Blount now works under a contract to write "many pieces of various kinds at nice rates," but the money comes only upon publication, which may be up to five months after acceptance. Humor produced from Blount's original ideas, as opposed to those suggested by editors from other magazines, goes to the *Atlantic* first. In 1989, his contract as a contributing editor with the magazine was in its eighth year.

Blount's steady production has made him "tired of cranking out so many things for magazines. . . . I've stopped keeping track of how many pieces I write a year, but it used to be thirty-something," he said. "For years it was a rare and unsettling experience to find nothing I'd written on a well-stocked newsstand at any given moment, and it wasn't unusual to find three or four things." Bibliographical guides do not accurately reflect Blount's production. By his count, he has averaged about twenty-five pieces a year since 1977, with a high in 1978 when he published seventeen magazine articles and seventeen columns in the *New York Times.* These publications have been in addition to other kinds of writing and public appearances.

His most unusual free-lance writing effort has been *It Grows on You: A Hair-raising Survey of Human Plumage,* a humorous study of American hirsuphilia, with photographs by Bob Adelman, published in 1986 as a 159-page slick paperback by the Dolphin division of Doubleday and Company. The book was poorly promoted, received little attention, and three years later was the only one of Blount's books that was out of print. No wonder: it is not the usual barber- and beauty-shop reading (and not gender specific either, though the female perspective dominates); it is not serious enough to be treated as informative, though it is; and it is not clearly organized. The author smartly compares the book's organization to hair: "Excuse this book, I know it's a mess. I mean verbally, structurally, deep down. Yes, I'm sure it does *look* nice; thank you. But if you only knew the thin spots, the cowlicks, the wandering parts, the *loss,* the stray leads. Things keep popping up!"

(10). Blount said that when publication terms between Adelman, who suggested the project, and the publisher were finally ironed out, after a contract had been signed and the money accepted, he had to write the book in ten days to make deadline.

Unlike most of Blount's other writings, *It Grows on You* required research, mainly the winnowing out of quotations about hair and the rounding up of interviews with hairdressers, barbers, shampoo manufacturers, women of various dispositions, and a few men. Among the quotations in the frontispiece are a snatch of dialogue between Parmenides and Socrates, part of the speech by Hamlet's ghost, and "Sometimes, you like to let the hair do the talking," by soul singer James Brown. The interviews and profiles offer a clear, often funny picture of the hairdressing scene, and the book builds to Blount's "hair theory of human evolution," according to which hominids got up and walked on two feet because "Man is the animal that is always trying to keep her hair out of her eyes. And out of her way generally. And failing" (145).

In a magazine or in a collection of essays, the piece would stand out; it parodies scientific speculation and image making and comes near the conclusion of a book dealing with an American social and commercial phenomenon that is anything but trivial. The "evolution" essay, however, is buried beneath the photographs (several of Blount, from high school to the present), the serious information, the boxed quotations, and the various flippancies. *It Grows on You* is a good illustration of Blount's skills as a reader, listener, writer, and conversational humorist; it is an even better demonstration of the mass-market setting in which literary humor is surest to fail.

Other writing efforts have been more financially successful than professionally satisfying. Blount was paid $50,000 for writing a remake of the Spencer Tracy–Katharine Hepburn movie *Pat and Mike,* another assignment that he finished in ten working days after mulling it over for a while. Blount turned in a first draft but the script never became a movie, because all the principals contracting with Blount were fired. He also wrote an original baseball script for Paramount for $17,500, a job he was talked into by Pauline Kael, the *New Yorker* movie critic, when she was briefly a developer of projects for Paramount. An independent producer who wanted to make a movie from the script was refused the rights from Paramount, Blount said. Another project put on hold was a TV pilot of a series to be based loosely on *What Men Don't Tell Women* and produced by a cable network.

Blount finds movie and TV writing "not gratifying work" and says his attitude toward money is like that of Ralph Touchett in Henry James's *Portrait of a Lady:* "It's a terrible thing to follow but a charming thing to meet."[7] (He has met enough of it to enable him to buy another house in Mill River, after his first was lost in the divorce settlement with Joan Ackermann, proceedings that were completed in 1989.)

Blount has been able to make a living doing what he wants to do— which is to write and perform humor. Although his off-Broadway show earned him only $125 a night, his lecture appearances, ranging to about ten a year, produce fees to his lecture agency (which keeps 20 percent) that average about $6,000-plus-expenses each, enough, Blount says, to give him more freedom to write. Despite his interest in the public performance of humor, even despite a bit part in Jonathan Demme's movie *Married to the Mob,* Blount has never become stage-struck. Listed as the "Humane Reporter" in the final credit roll, he is one of a gang of newsmen and asks a Mafia don, played by Dean Stockwell, who is emerging from a courtroom, "How are the feds treating you, Tony?" The result of his experience is a long first-person profile of Demme in *Esquire.*[8]

The writing of humor, and occasionally the expository essay, has continued to be Blount's life and his living. Book advances have increased with his reputation, rising to $60,000 for *Now, Where Were We?* Although the last four books have not earned back the advances (*It Grows on You* will not, since it is out of print), Blount estimates his annual royalty income from the collections at about $4,000. Since royalty income does not begin until a year after publication, that figure, as of 1989, did not include *Now, Where Were We?* Magazines pay Blount from $1.25 to $2.50 a word, sometimes more, Blount says, because of his "chronic semi-unavailability" and the aggressiveness of his agent, Esther Newberg.

Magazine editors, not agents, have suggested most of Blount's assignments. Pushed on by his "desperation," Blount has been able to provide satisfactory work on time. "As a former college puller-of-all-nighters and newspaper reporter, I can write fast when I have to," he said. "But I rewrite obsessively. I am motivated by a longing (and economic necessity) to be finished and by a fear that what I am about to set down will be as unreadable as what I have just finished setting down." He had no agent for *About Three Bricks Shy of a Load;* the contract, with an advance of $30,000 (half of which went to *Sports Illustrated* to pay living and entertainment expenses), was negotiated by an assistant managing editor at *Sports Illustrated*. Blount's contract with *Crackers* was negotiated by Liz Darhansoff of International Famous, an agency name that appealed to Blount because it sounded "just about tawdry enough"; all book deals thereafter have been handled by Newberg of the ICM agency.

In fifteen years of free lancing, Blount has learned the downside:

All your vacations are either working or unpaid, you have to finance your own word processor, you have no Xerox machine, you have to schlep things down to the post office, and you probably work at home, which means that neither you nor anyone else really feels that you are in a workplace. You are of course your own boss, but that takes all the fun out of goofing off, at least per se. And it generally takes longer for a publishing empire to write your check than it took you to write your article. Editors, who may do a little writing themselves for *extra* money, never quite get it that these checks are it for you. And while you are waiting for your check and trying to concentrate on several other assignments, you keep getting calls from editors wanting you to add thirty lines or cut forty-seven or from fact-checkers wanting to know who this Louis Armstrong you refer to is or where they can go to verify that Matthew Arnold ever referred to armies as ignorant.

As eloquent as Blount may be in describing the frenzy and the anxiety of free-lance writing, he is also aware of the advantages it has offered—not simply the independence but also the opportunity to come into direct literary and commercial contact with magazine and book publishing, editors' prerogatives, movie and television writing, literary agencies, and the lecture circuit. On a deeper level, free lancing informs Blount's humor; it is, itself, an arena, or pulpit, or playing field. The editor provides a primary audience and a primary tension, forcing decisions about what is likely to be funny and to whom; the tug between writer and editor suggests the more fundamental conflict between integrity and economic necessity. Obviously stimulated by the exchanges, on every level, Blount has converted the tensions into humor; his position as a free-lancer is, in fact, the sine qua non of his identity as a detached but not wholly independent observer of the world.

Blount's productivity over a fifteen-year period indicates that he has not been ground down by the drudgeries and insecurities. Though he may gnash at the shortcomings of free-lance writing and recall crises when compromise threatened, he has resisted switching entirely from humor writing to more lucrative movie and television scriptwriting and acting, a reluctance that keeps him from following too closely in the footsteps of Robert Benchley. From his base as a free-lancer, Blount has found and cultivated relationships with such prominent magazines as *Sports Illustrated, Esquire,* and *Atlantic,* and the *New Yorker* and, in so doing, has attracted the attention of other seekers after his humor—editors, book publishers, television producers, lecture planners, readers, and fans. Beginning with *About Three Bricks Shy of a Load,* when he was still nominally a staff writer at *Sports Illustrated,* Blount has steadily and willfully shaped his career, or, as he calls it, his "franchise." The development of that franchise—a financial and literary enterprise that has resulted from a combination of talent, energy, determination, diplomacy, and consistent good luck—may be studied by an explication of those books which contain the best of Roy Blount's magazine writing and which have formed his reputation as a literary humorist.

Chapter Four
Literary Sportswriting:
About Three Bricks Shy of a Load

He took a pass in the right flat, all the way over by the right side-line, and cut back toward the other side. As tackler after tackler slanted into him he moved, fending them off, in a series of slues—looking for a gap to cut up through, never finding it, but always advancing somewhat on each swoop, moving downfield gradually, gradually, bevelly, bevelly, rhythmically, like a handsaw, *ooo*-fah, *ooo*-fah into hard wood—all the way across the field diagonally and out of bounds on the other side, to stop the clock. A 15-second 13-yard gain with a serrated edge.
     —Roy Blount, Jr.'s description of a run by Franco Harris, in *About Three Bricks Shy of a Load*

With the 1974 publication of *About Three Bricks Shy of a Load*[1] (with its long, misleading trailer of a subtitle: "A Highly Irregular Lowdown on the Year the Pittsburgh Steelers Were Super but Missed the Bowl"), Roy Blount, Jr., felt his first wave of national adulation—not as a humorist but as a sportswriter. Praise came from major newspapers across the country for his account of a season spent, from training camp through the single play-off game, living and "loafing," a Pittsburgh term for carousing, with the 1973 players. Blount was described in the *New York Times Book Review* as "bright and sensitive," "tough and tal-ented," and "exceptionally gifted"; the reviewer added that "no other book explains so well the paradox of the brutality and subtlety of this repelling and fascinating game."[2] When the first installments of the book appeared in *Sports Illustrated* in the summer of 1974, a Pittsburgh reviewer described Blount's writing as "tough, honest, true."[3] The *Wall Street Journal* praised Blount's use of language as reflecting "his appreciation of nuance and sound in the voices he listened to from July to January."[4] The *Baltimore Sun* reviewer described the book as "far and away the best nonfiction account of professional football since *Paper Lion*," but noted that because of "charm, grace and wit" in the writing,

Blount also reminded him of A. J. Liebling.[5] In a blurb on the back cover of the 1980 paperback reprint, Dan Jenkins, the author of the pro football novel *Semi-tough* and Blount's former colleague at *Sports Illustrated,* commended the book as "a literary and journalistic masterpiece."

Unlike much other sports journalism, Blount's book about the Pittsburgh Steelers has not staled. Jonathan Yardley, who gave the book a paragraph in a gang review in *Sports Illustrated* in 1974, cited it in his 1982 roster of the country's ten best sports books—a list that included Ring Lardner's *You Know Me, Al* but not Plimpton's *Paper Lion.*[6] Part of the initial popularity of *About Three Bricks Shy of a Load* is due, of course, to the existence of millions of potential readers of any new book on professional athletics, but the success of Blount's book has persisted long past a seasonal interest. It was published in a new edition, and with new material, in November 1989 under the title *About Three Bricks Shy of a Load . . . and the Load Filled Up.* Despite the praise and popularity, the reason for the durability of Blount's book in a sports-saturated age is still not readily apparent.

In fact, it is much easier to compare *About Three Bricks Shy of a Load* with other sports books than it is to define its uniqueness. Unlike George Plimpton, who lived out a Walter Mitty fantasy by scrimmaging with a pro team, Blount does not depend on a clever angle or make the humiliation of the writer a comic necessity. Nor is his book a veiled exposé of the inanity, violence, and pathos of professional football, as is Dan Jenkins's *Semi-tough.* Blount does not make the Pittsburgh Steelers a synecdoche for all of professional sports or attempt to show that the sport is a mirror of a national madness. The book is a calculated study of surfaces, those of the entire Pittsburgh Steeler phenomenon and those of the narrator-essayist himself. Although the book is written in the first person and influenced by the popularity of New Journalism, whatever Blount says about himself in it serves the book more than the man, or the subject more than the writer; no attempt is made to point up the importance of the book or the perspicacity of the writer. The book is not *critical,* in the particular or even the general sense; no single thesis appears to guide Blount toward a paraphrasable point. Moreover, the book provides little information that a reader could not, or would not, have gotten elsewhere in the sports-saturated media; nor does it offer the kind of expert analysis that sportscasters call color. Whatever gossip is passed along in the course of the narrative neither scandalizes nor enlightens.

What, then, accounts for this book's vitality and its role in the shaping of Blount's reputation and career? Jenkins was close to the mark in applying the term *literary*. In *About Three Bricks Shy of a Load,* Blount was able to sustain a literary voice throughout a book composed primarily of essays joined by brief accounts of actual football games; but, more importantly, he was able to define and convert to his own purposes, in a continuous, dynamic process, the problem faced by every writer lodged between readers and famous living persons of any profession.

Simply put, how is the writer to place himself with respect to his subject? To establish and preserve the integrity of the writer when the aim is neither to deflate the subject in order to inflate the observer (the essential Howard Cosell mode) nor to hype the subject and humble the observer (the standard role for local sportswriters called, usually in scorn, homers) requires writing skills best described in the same terms applied successful athletes and coaches: ingenuity, stamina, strategy, and, not the least, courage. A writer who sets out to criticize or to compliment avoids the problem altogether. Objectivity is an illusion of such writing, even though facts may be verified and both sides of any given controversy can be presented; the message to the reader or viewer is that the writer or sportscaster is, from the outset, either superior or inferior to the subject. Although it is arguable whether any sports reporting can be objective, Blount's writing demonstrates that a different kind of engagement is possible, that a writer can be level with his subject and gain an access to the subject in a way not open to the gadflies or homers. Although the great distance between the subject and the writer can never be bridged, and the dilemma created by the disparity between the magnitude of the subject and the puny voice of the writer never really removed, Blount takes advantage of the inherent conflict by using it as a foundation for his writing. The structure and the style depend on the tensions between the subject and the writer; the book succeeds because Blount was able to use those tensions to depict, in a manner and at a level probably outside the reach (and certainly outside the practice) of television journalism, how a professional football player's life differs from Everyfan's.

Two initial facts influenced the style and structure of *About Three Bricks Shy of a Load:* it started with an idea from André Laguerre, the managing editor of *Sports Illustrated,* and it required the cooperation of the Steeler front office and coaching staff. In the opening chapter,

Blount explains the circumstances under which he wrote the book and indicates that the exposition will be gentle. "Pro football players are adults who fly through the air in plastic helmets and smash each other for a living," he writes in the first sentence. "I now know a bunch of them, and I think they are good folks" (1). Before the opening chapter is finished, Blount's position as less than a scourge but more than a supplicant is also defined. After a Whitmanesque catalog of what constitutes a football player, Blount mentions the "rich penumbra" of the sport and describes watching a game from the sidelines as "like standing in the eye of a tumbler washing machine, only noise and throat-figures all around instead of soapsuds and clothes" (1). The vocabulary, the metaphors, and the allusions and references to a particular world outside of sports will, in fact, separate if not elevate the writer, though without the condescension of a Cosell—and without the witless malapropisms. Blount's tone is never supercilious; he takes no cheap shots; and he makes it clear that he is not gratifying an author's ego at the expense of the subject. If, as a writer, he has a separate vocabulary, he also speaks the players' language. Blount quotes the sideline conversation with reserve defensive end Craig Hanneman that resulted in the book's title: "You picked the right team! Oh, a great bunch guys! And a bunch of crazy fuckers! We're all about three bricks shy of a load!" (2).

Blount has his own crazy energy—the hours to spend listening to locker-room talk and the liver to stand the beer-and-shots of Pittsburgh bars—but if *load* refers to the intelligence and education necessary to write about a world as complicated as pro football, the writer must be less shy of a load than his subjects. If, however, *load* also implies authority, or power over the subject, Blount starts where any other sports fan would, more than three bricks off. In the course of explaining the background for the book, Blount defines the rhetorical problem:

I came into sportswriting unexpectedly from a newspaper job in which I made fun of, and occasionally deigned to talk to, politicians. I was the natural man, the politicians were the connivers. I was primary, they were secondary. In sportswriting I found it to be the other way around: the athletes were instinctive artists, just trying to stay inspired and exercise their craft, and I was in the position of trying to get them to conceptualize, to say something that they tended to feel would somehow get them into social, financial or ontological trouble. I will never entirely get over the sensation of realizing that my boyhood idol Willie Mays disliked me on sight. The fact that every other writer I know who ever tried to talk to Mays came away with the same impression does not really help. "Willie," I said to him at one point, "do you realize that the last eight innings you've led off, you've gotten on base seven times?" "Man," he said, "I don't keep up with that shit." (5)

The anecdote serves well. The humiliation creates a challenge for the writer, who has to regain some confidence in himself. The language also implies the presence of a particular reader, one intelligent enough to identify with the writer, to realize that however great Mays may be he still needs that writer, and to be grateful that the writer is in the social and rhetorical position to absorb the rebuke for the reader. The Mays incident also gives the writer an opportunity to earn the reader's respect through his own performance:

All I want to happen to me in heaven is for Willie Mays to come up to me and say, by no means humbly, but appreciatively, "Do you realize that in the last eight descriptive sentences you've written you've used only one adjective?" "Man," I will say (*nicely,* but firmly), "I don't keep up with that shit." (5–6)

By the conclusion of the second chapter, Blount has established a persona and style that the reader recognizes as necessary for access to whatever story might follow. The writer brings to the rhetorical pivot a literary sensibility, not overly proud of its intelligence, schooling, and keen eye but also not surrendering to the magnitude of the subject. Irreverent but still friendly, bold though never secure, the writer can observe and empathize yet remain an alien. The limitations of the camaraderie are reflected in a prose style that draws on the trashy talk of the locker room, accepted as a standard for all exchanges between the subjects and the writer (who knows how to hand a four-letter word back to Willie Mays), but talk that is superseded by the narrator's vocabulary. (No football player says *penumbra* or even *ontological.*) The writer obviously has liberties and skills not possessed by his subjects; through language he merges with and emerges from his subject; without flaunting the fact, he can—perhaps *must*—show that in the world of often dumb but always powerful jocks, his perspective and education have produced a higher appreciation of their lives. More importantly, the style also allows the writer to be, at once, an objective narrator, a subjective essayist, and an autobiographer; with these various roles at his disposal, he can use himself as a point of reference, yet resist letting his story steal the book.

This movement between the subject and the self, between a subject worthy of attention and a first-person speaker who is both observer and participant, provides the tension in a story essentially without suspense. In the unlikely event that some naive reader of the middle 1970s might stumble upon the book not knowing about the Steelers' last season before the string of Super Bowl victories (or perhaps in anticipation of the long life of the book), the outcome is told in the first chapter. Although the Steelers had a respectable 10–4 record and showed the promise that would be fulfilled the following year, the season was without the kind of "immaculate reception"—the last-second catch by Franco Harris that extended the Steelers' 1972 play-off hopes by one game— that made the previous year memorable. Writing during and directly after the season (parts of the book were published in *Sports Illustrated*), Blount offered no predictions; nor did he, in the preface to the 1980 paperback, make himself out as prescient. The refusal to indulge, even humorously, in hindsight is conspicuous, suggesting that Blount intended a literary work that would stand on its own, without the need for pragmatic justification.

A key to the independence and durability of *About Three Bricks Shy of a Load* is the dearth of on-the-field action presented. Of the thirty chapters, only seven of the briefest deal directly with the games. Defeats of the Lions, the Browns, and the Oilers, for instance, are handled in one five-page chapter. The scarcity of play-by-play narration is more than a concession to television or newspapers. The real action in the book is social. Characters are presented against their backgrounds as athletes, family men, and representatives of racial or ethnic histories, and they live in a world almost as narrow and as literary—and, in a comic way, as doomed—as that of *The Pequod*. As an Ishmael, the narrator observes players living within two kinds of confinement: within Pittsburgh and the team and within the boundaries of their own brief, violent professional lives. The sense of time and place present in the writing transcends the superficial and provides the serious, hidden foundation for essays on names, principal players, Pittsburgh itself, the coach, fans, the team owner, the premises, race, scouting, money, and hands. Even the cryptic chapters describing game action function primarily as narrative transitions between expository essays.

The social context of pro football is put in perspective by the writer's use of literary and political contexts, though he introduces them too

casually to appear pretentious or pompous. Epigraphs used to introduce the chapters come from, among others, Blount's children, James
Boswell, John Keats, Frenchy Fuqua, and W. C. Fields. ("Ah yes;
beanbag. Becomes very exciting at times. I saw the world champion-
ships in Paris. Several people were killed.") The higher literary references do not suffer in the low company, the irreverence in fact
suggesting reverence; instead, specific references sprinkled throughout
the prose serve the exposition by continually reintroducing the serious
and comic literary context. In the early chapter on the Steelers' presea-
son training camp—the longest essay in the book—Blount describes a
rookie whose expression betrays his dislike of football; in the player's
dour look and thinning hair Blount sees a reflection of himself when
he was in his own training camp, the Graduate English Department
of Harvard University, in a class conducted by the famous scholar
I. A. Richards: "I saw Richards nearly swoon, literally, from reading
Shelley. I remember thinking, I *like* literature and all, but . . . " (109).
A literary frame also defines the character of the unclubbable head
coach, Chuck Noll, nicknamed for obvious reasons the Pope, who
functions as a foil to the sociable, verbal writer. A separate chapter
deals more directly with Noll, but Blount's initial apprehension of the
coach in training camp is expressed in a literary context. "I could seldom think of anything to say that would *advance* a discussion with
Noll," he wrote. Then he draws on the Henry Adams essay "The Dynamo and the Virgin" (though he switches the nouns) to muse that the
owner of the Steelers since 1933, the venerable Art Rooney, represented the Virgin, who had inspired cathedrals, and that the more
impersonal Noll was the Dynamo, the force that drove the future.
With Noll, the literary references serve another purpose: they call attention away from the concessions required of a sportswriter granted
so many liberties; when Noll gives Blount the social stiff-arm, the
writer can resort to another context in which to describe the coach.
Without the literary references, what would he have but his own subjective, arbitrary impressions to advance the essay? Returning to
Adams later in the training camp chapter, Blount again uses the at-
tractive, benumbing power of the Dynamo to explain his relationship
with Noll, who did not want his team, described by Blount as "not an
open society" but "a society at war," stirred up or interfered with in
the advance upon the Super Bowl: "In his researches into the Dynamo,
said Henry Adams of himself in the third person, he 'mixed himself
up in the tangle of ideas until he achieved a sort of Paradise of igno-

rance vastly consoling to his fatigued senses. He wrapped himself in vibrations and rays which were new . . . while he lost his arithmetic in trying to figure out the equation between the discoveries and economies of force. The economics, like the discoveries, were absolute, supernatural, occult; incapable of expression in horse power'" (85). Dropped in without a pedantic explication, the Adams reference is ambiguous. If Blount himself is identifying with Adams, he confesses that Noll, the Dynamo, is a powerful enigma, beyond the reach of language. If, however, Noll is being identified with Henry Adams, in his "Paradise of ignorance" and enamored of the Dynamo, what he lacks is the ability to express power in terms understandable to fans, to readers, and maybe to players. If so, what Noll's preoccupation with power requires is a person capable of expression—namely a writer, namely Blount—to serve as the opposite pole.

However central the literary references may be, they are used sparingly and strategically, as an occasional reinforcement. The writing is not subordinate to other literature, nor is the literary context used reductively. A professional football season might well lend itself to a lampoon or a mock epic, but Blount makes no attempt to lower his subjects. And for the most part, the literature is used openly, to further the exposition, and through direct reference rather than allusion. If the shading is subtle, it is no less significant. It inserts into Blount's own literary equation a force different from and more powerful than football—one capable of ranging across thought and time—yet in this crazy, three-bricks-shy-of-a-load context, a force dominated by the limitations of the sport. Rather than literature patronizing football, the opposite actually is taking place: Henry Adams may have been bright enough to coach the Pittsburgh Steelers. Juxtaposing the disparate but converging worlds appeals to readers familiar with both and capable of appreciating the use of great writers to revivify a genre often made moribund by clichés. The appeal to the power of literature is so critical to Blount's rhetoric that rarely does he lapse into an overclever use of it, though he occasionally will yield to the temptation to pun. In an allusion that only a reader familiar with William Butler Yeats's "The Second Coming" would understand, Blount reaches for the most famous verse in the poem to describe the role of a certain offensive lineman who insists that despite the sharp eyes of the referees he can avoid being penalized for holding: "Things fall apart, if the center cannot hold" (336).

About Three Bricks Shy of a Load depends on Blount's literary knowledge and on the highly selected use of literary skills, in particular his ability to write vernacular narration. The exposition, for instance, is marked by a virtual absence of concrete descriptions of individuals. Physical details that might provide connotations, implying judgments of the people, are conspicuously absent; the definitions of character instead come primarily through dialogue and anecdote, supported by the commentary of the narrator. Even in the chapter in which the players are introduced, no attempt is made to use other techniques to distinguish the players. As a result of this calculated omission, the players are largely responsible for defining themselves. For the most part, they speak in one language: jocktalk. This combination of juvenile name-calling, anxious jostling, obscenity (almost no profanity), and the verbal facility to create figurative language and to tell stories puts the lie to the implicit contention that talking about football ranks so far below playing it that language deserves little direct attention. Yet for all the excellent talk, the image left of the players is, because of the lack of descriptive details distinguishing individuals, largely abstract. Jefferson Street Joe Gilliam's erratic play, Frenchy Fuqua's posings, Andy Russell's shrewd off-the-field entrepreneurship, Jon Kolb's desire to have a farm—all are handled as sensations of the team, important in any given moment but ephemeral. The individual players are not merely subordinate to the owner, the coach, and, of course, the impressions of the writer; they are also representative characters, defined by the ethos of pro football.

That context had to be examined, and Blount had his own test to pass, if the book was not to be dismissed as trivial. Obviously he was not afraid to expose—yes, there is a discussion of the size of penises revealed in the locker room (no names, no measurements)—but the greater courage was required for a look at less physical issues. In 1973, when the sports pages carried stories about Franco Harris's injury and Mean Joe Greene's prowess on defense, the front pages were full of Watergate news. Noll's favoring of Haldeman and Erlichman in the political game of 1973 gets an occasional mention, but Blount holds the analogy in check. Less specific but far more important is the matter of race.

Blount includes a racial identification for each player in the chapter on names, and he devotes a short essay to the subject in a chapter that opens with an epigraph quoting a letter to *Sports Illustrated:* "Please stop my subscription. I have had just about all the colored people stuffed down my throat I can stand" (289). How important was race to the Steelers and, by extension, to professional athletics? Blounts lets exposition answer the question:

[T]here were differences between being a black Steeler and being a white one. One afternoon there were steaks in front of the lockers of several white Steelers—honoraria for their appearance at the Duquesne Club to chat with the members. Frenchy, Franco and Joe Greene were in demand for public appearances, but most of the other blacks were overlooked. In four years, Mel Blount had had one autograph session. Hardly any of the blacks made the business contacts that the whites who wanted to did. The blacks were more likely than the whites to be preyed upon by the people who, as Gilliam put it, "seem sincere and all the time they're planning to fuck your mama and blow you up too." (290)

The commitment to exposition allows the writer to recount all that he sees and knows—which, effectively, precludes sentimentality and editorial self-righteousness. Even though blacks themselves define the racial problem, raising the issue nevertheless puts the white writer at some risk. Blount approaches the subject without blinking or rationalizing. He tells of a scouting trip to black colleges on which he saw entire teams fighting, fans encroaching to the thirty-yard line, and two opposing head coaches "come rolling out onto the field, tearing each other's shirts to ribbons, over the question of whether the ball should be striped or not" (291–92). Blount considers this behavior a positive contribution to the game. He also discusses the physical differences between white and black athletes; however, whereas Jimmy the Greek paid the price for his 1988 comments on national television, Blount, publishing more than a decade earlier, could escape the charges of prejudice by avoiding half-baked historical theories and by refusing to be absolutely serious. One swift sentence exemplifies his ability to confront the issue and convert it: "Black athletes look and move better than white ones on the average. I don't see anything invidious about the belief that black people have longer Achilles tendons than whites (which means, as a friend of mine once pointed out, that Ethel Waters can jump higher than Kate Smith)" (292).

As a white Southerner sharing a name with a fellow Georgian, Mel Blount, the great all-pro defensive back who happened to be black, Roy Blount could claim a regional, historical, and linguistic kinship with the blacks—an important rhetorical advantage. But he remains safely in the middle, a listener more than a talker. Criticisms of the

pro football system and of the Pittsburgh management are brief and
oblique. He points out that assertive black prospects, unlike their
white counterparts, are called "militant" and that John Rowser, an
abrasive talker who had had a shouting match with assistant coach Bud
Carson, was traded to Denver. "Let's don't tell him," Carson said.
"Let's make him read about it in the papers" (291). In the world Blount
has presented, race is a fact, and it suffuses almost everything done by
the Steelers; showing that the issue could be presented as levelly as
everything else in the book is evasive but also sufficient, the author
implies. Like the rhetorical problem presented by Blount's own relationship with the subjects, the racial tension is capable of conversion
into a form of energy.

About Three Bricks Shy of a Load depends so greatly upon Blount's
skills as an essayist that the final chapter, which might, given the
structure suggested by the season, emphasize the disappointment of
the play-off defeat, becomes merely a signing-off until the next training camp. Of course there was no indication that the book would conclude with any suspense; the penultimate chapter was entitled
"Hands," a long study of their importance in several aspects of the
game, opening with quotations from Gorky on Tolstoy, from Flannery
O'Connor, and from a newspaper account of a fundamentalist snake
handler in Tennessee. At the conclusion of the book, with its world-
without-end tone, it is evident that in the account of the Steelers' year
Blount has been not simply the author but also the authority. He was
not bound by the dictates of the season, the coaches, the owners, the
fans, or even his readers. As an essayist in the tradition of Montaigne,
he was, in the literal sense, trying the team out on his own terms.

In the last chapter, Blount calls himself "the detached scribe," a
prophetic description. With the publication of the book, he left the
regular employment of Sports Illustrated and, as Ring Lardner had done
earlier in the century, started to slough off the label of sportswriter.
No doubt had he continued he would have been forced to repeat himself. By never attempting to reduce his subjects directly, by rarely criticizing (and then making certain not to enjoy being critical), by
withholding concrete descriptions of his subjects, and by constantly
reminding the reader of the gulf between the professional athlete and
the sportswriter, Blount demonstrated completely the rhetoric of modern sportswriting. He adopted a literary perspective that allowed him
to write about the whole phenomenon of pro football from within and
from without and that also gave him the greatest latitude in speaking

to the reader. Furthermore, he proved that he was up to the task; he exhibited the facility—the energy, the empathy, and the wit—of a literary man able to create the rhetorical form and fill it with content.

Blount's command of the language—which includes his ability to conceal that command—puts him in the class of the writer under whose name he received the Vanderbilt scholarship, Grantland Rice. Affecting the low style rather than the high, Blount was still able to set sports in a dignified context and to give the sportswriter a distinctive voice. Although Blount is no longer thought of primarily as a sportswriter, his achievement in *About Three Bricks Shy of a Load* is remembered; when commentators are sought to explain the phenomenon of pro football, Blount is still in demand. In the NFL Films television documentary "Autumn Ritual," produced by Steve Sabol in 1986, Blount compared former Steeler wide receiver Lynn Swann with Mikhail Baryshnikov: "I'd like to see Baryshnikov dance while people are trying to stop him and separate his head from his body." Contained in the comparison, as it had been in the book, is the implication that sports exists in contrast to other worlds, in a separate, significant, but not necessarily superior context.

The conclusion of *About Three Bricks Shy of a Load* (which turned out to be much more than simply an "irregular lowdown") foreshadows the end of *Crackers*. Backing away from a summary judgment, letting observation override criticism, Blount leaves his material where he had found it, claiming no influence over the season and no completeness for the book. The players have not lost respect for themselves or the game; they, and the writer, have survived and will be ready for another season. The final two sentences come from a conversation with the all-pro linebacker Andy Russell: "It's a great game. It's not like going to play a game of squash" (355). The understatement is a final indication of how much control Blount could exercise over himself, his material, and his craft.

Chapter Five

The Humorist and the President: *Crackers*

Still, I have had a hard time figuring out what he has been up to, overall. He is from *my own state* and I have trouble telling where he is coming from!
—From "The Invocation" to *Crackers*

By the fourth year of Jimmy Carter's presidency, the national press was in full cry; Carter's competence was questioned and his reelection doubtful. Roy Blount's fellow Georgian, who entered office as the avatar of honesty, was setting the Gallup public-approval record with a rating lower than Richard Nixon's at its lowest; the Lou Harris poll reported that "on no single issue does Carter have a majority of voters who stand up and say they like him."[1] An assessment of the Carter presidency in August 1980 by *Time* political correspondent Hugh Sidey, not known for savaging liberal Democratic presidents, turned out to be typically mealymouthed. Evaluating the president on the eve of the Democrats' nominating convention, Sidey started with a comment on the president's nationally televised effort to explain how he would handle Billy Carter's controversial dealings with the Libyans: "It was the best of Carter, a profoundly caring man, loving his brother through stress, as honest as a politician knows how to be, skillfully projecting his concern from his electronic stage to an estimated 65 million Americans. He was forceful in his conviction of his own rectitude and master of every detail in the intricate caper of Billy, the wily and greedy buffoon." Without stating so flatly, Sidey moved toward the incontrovertible conclusion that, although Jimmy Carter's goodness had not eroded ("As a symbol of personal integrity and candor he is undimmed"), he was so incompetent and confusing as president that everybody from Lesley Stahl to the Soviets was bumfuzzled.[2]

While middle-of-the-road commentators like Sidey were wallowing in qualifiers, conservatives were on the wide road toward Reagan's "city on the hill." Richard Brookhiser, breezing along in the October issue of the *National Review,* observed "a conservative tide gathering out beyond the reefs" that Carter was powerless to stem; moreover, he identified Carter with one of the president's own catchwords—*malaise*—and recalled how Carter had defined the term in his July 1979 speech on the energy question: "a growing doubt about the meaning of our lives and a loss of unity of purpose for our nation." Although Brookhiser did point out that Carter's record "only reflected the limitations of a spiritually baffled citizenry," he resurrected Barry Goldwater's 1964 "vice-and-virtue" rhetoric to delight in the Democrats' dilemma in having to choose Carter over Ted Kennedy, a choice between "the millionaire playboy who practices vice only when it hurts him" and "the born-again Christian who preaches virtue only when it helps him."[3]

Jimmy Carter was the tar-baby president—everything hurled at him stuck—and yet, for all his vulnerability, he continued to mystify an electorate that could not come to terms with his virtue, his intelligence, his vacillations, and, most importantly, his Southernness. The Carter presidency invited criticism, even condemnation, but it resisted definitive analysis from left, right, and center. If the press accounts indicate a consensus, most voters still did not understand Carter or his milieu, could not view the presidency from a national and a Southern perspective, and did not realize that the Carter phenomenon could be approached through humor.

Even among the political cartoonists, the daily columnists, and the talk-show comedians, little was made of the humor in the White House. At a panel discussion sponsored by the American Humor Studies Association in Washington one year after Carter was elected, Art Buchwald said, "People are getting pretty bored with Billy Carter and Amy. I don't find Carter all that fascinating either." Jeff MacNelly, the cartoonist who put Jimmy on the front porch of many a dilapidated country service station, said, "When Carter came to office, it was like one of my cartoons came to life. But the image gets very dull after a while." Mark Russell was not ready to give up on the Carter administration, but he found the Carter issues poor sources of humor.[4] Jimmy Carter was, after all, a serious candidate and a serious president; he came to office when the country wanted a clean, righteous outsider. The president's retinue of Georgians and sundry Southerners endured their cheap shots and suffered their scandals, though nobody was convicted of anything and most rumors were unconfirmed; nevertheless, the Carter administration generally enjoyed the respect due mystery.

A pageant of stereotypes—not simply Billy, a humorist's delight—

never developed into a spectacle of humor. Perhaps it was the power of the office, or the religious conviction of the president, or the country's desire to make Miss Lillian into a Southern Rose Kennedy that forestalled all but the crudest of jokes. ("Who has the two largest boobs in America? Miss Lillian—Billy and Jimmy!") In fact, to more than a few Southerners, it appeared that Jimmy might have worked a joke on the country. The president had done enough maneuvering in his race for the governorship, and during it, to raise the normal suspicions of a successful politician's purity. One Georgia legislator told a network reporter, "He's anybody's dog that'll hunt with him." A letter to the *Atlanta Constitution* editor before the election described Carter as "a New York liberal with a Southern accent," and the mayor of Macon, a former Republican gubernatorial candidate, showed that two-party politics, Southern style, had arrived in Georgia when he called Carter "the biggest liar in the country."[5] Despite all the local rhetoric, the image of the president as a canny, possibly shady politician did not become part of his national image.

Just how difficult the problem of perceiving the Carters was—and just how far some analysts would go to be serious and profound—is reflected in *Jimmy Carter and American Fantasy,* which is probably the most unintentionally hilarious study of any U.S. president and his family. Five psychohistorians turned their perceptions and their reflexive rationalizings on the Carters just before the 1976 election. Typical was Paul H. Elovitz, who spent three days in Plains absorbing the Carter phenomenon, studying surfaces and drawing mock-epic conclusions. He discovers a Jimmy Carter diary from Annapolis days and notes that the Georgia midshipman described cutting his gums one morning on a piece of hard toast and being pleased that the injury kept him from having to speak at mess. Conclusion: Carter might have a "self-destructive streak." Miss Lillian invites the visitor to her house and forces some Twinkies on him ("Protestations about my diet were unavailing"), apologizes that her TV is only black-and-white, says she hates beer but offers him one left by a security man anyway (repeating that she hates beer), and forces him to endure "comparable episodes." Conclusion: "I did not feel comfortable, and found myself wondering what the effect of this kind of continuous ambivalence could be on one's children."[6]

Although Miss Lillian was a remarkable, resilient woman—a Peace Corps volunteer nurse in India during her seventies—her everyday Georgia behavior fell well within the norm for a Southern grandmother whose son was the Democrats' candidate for president of the United States and whose home was being overrun by psychohistorians. Yet as even these absurd analyses demonstrate, Jimmy Carter of Georgia was an outsider from one campaign to the next, though as an incumbent alien his status had shifted from positive and provincial to negative and national. Implied in the studies of Carter by the press and by the academicians is the general enigma of his identity as an American; he had become the center of a phenomenon (everyone wanted to make his rise to power a complex of characters and forces) that was nebulous, troubling, and indicative—but of what?

Sensing that the mood of inquiry turned on the "whole many-angled thing" of the Carter presidency, Roy Blount, Jr., read the context of the times and assembled a set of essays, several rewritten from magazine pieces, that envelop the Carter enigma in humor. Although on one level Blount's humor is a parody of political analysis, he explores the salient points of the Carter phenomenon and, along the way, establishes a perspective on the presidency, the South, and the nation. He also demonstrates how the humorist, as opposed to the satirist, can reduce material, yet somehow become it, leaving it undiminished.

Crackers: This Whole Many-angled Thing of Jimmy, More Carters, Ominous Little Animals, Sad-singing Women, My Daddy and Me purports to follow a steady progress of reduction—first of the writer himself, who confesses that he is wrestling with a subject too big for his humor, thus eluding the trap of sanctimoniousness and self-congratulation awaiting most analysts. Blount hears a "voice," compounded of coaches, teachers, sergeants, and the Old Testament, that reminds him of his inadequacy. Expressed in unmistakable, often all-uppercase italics, the voice returns occasionally throughout the humor to challenge the humorist and keep him humble. Blount also summons up a national constituency of Carter "relatives" from across the nation who form a chorus between the essays. In addition to revealing that Blount is not about to let his analysis become serious (and to showing that he is a master of vernacular narration), the caricatures in "More Carters" stand in contrast to their famous relative, who is sui generis, anything but a stereotype, and not likely to be reduced by an analyst, especially a humorist.

Although Blount uses other, less subtle means to call attention to Jimmy Carter's failure to satisfy the nation's need for a president voters can identify with, much less identify as a type, the interludes turn the humorist's powers of ridicule on totally fictional characters. Handling his major subjects with respect, Blount does not lampoon the president or any member of his family or administration. Hesitant to rise above his material, he alludes to the never-substantiated rumor of Hamilton Jordan's use of cocaine at Studio 54 and mentions Jody Powell's "flip" attitude, but he does not exploit some of the well-publicized incidents that seem inherently humorous. Not a word is said, for instance, about Sally Quinn's report that Jordan, after getting "fortified" at a state dinner, peered into an Egyptian woman's décolletage and said he had always wanted to see the pyramids.[7]

Blount's angle of vision is elevated enough for him to sit in judgment but not so high that he condescends. For the first time in his humor, Blount uses the Yankee-Southerner/Puritan-Cavalier routine developed as early as the 1850s by Joseph Glover Baldwin in *The Flush Times of Alabama and Mississippi*. Though he approaches the role of stage Southerner, Blount never fully assumes it and artfully dodges entrapment by it. Aware of the closure such role-playing involves, and aware that the territory for Southern humor was largely occupied either by writers of bloated, exaggerated descriptions to please the Northern grandstand (Florence King, Willie Morris) or by comedians who only had a Southern shtick (Brother Dave Gardner, Jerry Clower), Blount never swells into the fully vernacular persona, with a single voice. He is metaphorically but not solely a Cracker and can therefore accept or reject the label as it suits him in his treatment of the paradox of allegiance and alienation.

Like Jimmy Carter, the persona in *Crackers* is caught up in ambivalence, compelled to justify a regional identity to a national audience and needful of both a Southern and an American voice. He acknowledges the function of each in dealing with the uncomforting circumstances forced on him by the Carter presidency. For one, he is not defending the South on home turf; he is a Georgian, living in Massachusetts with a Northern-born spouse. Moreover, he feels, if not the burden of Southern history, then at least the need to explain and defend the South, even while obscuring and attacking it, and, furthermore, to defend himself against clichéd and false, intellectually smelly "explanations" of the South. It is a tight comic bind: but for the presidency of Jimmy Carter and the maundering of the national media, the humor implies, there would be no need for raising the question of sectional contrasts; however, since the issue has been revived, something must be made of it. The positioning of the persona with respect to the Southern identity is crucial: the humorist must be able to slip into the role of Southerner without being trapped by it, and, when out of the role, must not seem hypocritical and treasonous. Said another way, for the humor to work, the writer must be neither a stage Southerner nor a kept Southerner, reconstructed into a supercilious Yankee expatriate.

The posture of the humorist is established in the first essay, "Pissing and Moaning," in which Blount praises compost, "the kind of born-again we can all believe in—Vigoro out of corruption." He concedes that Southerners are full of compost and believes that the nation should be enriched by the Carter presidency; however, the chances of such a fertilization are slim for a person from Georgia rising to power "when the most sweeping program is 'Laverne and Shirley.'" The humorist, defining his audience as national and Southern, and not allowing the South to take the blame for the nation's direction, creates himself as a person caught in the middle—between issues, sections, and opinions. If the humorist wants to "assail" the president, it is not because Carter is a Southerner but because such criticism is a national prerogative, "what a president is for" (13). As an opening, "Pissing and Moaning" sends a clear signal: Blount, a Georgian, is not embarking on yet another tiresome and clichéd exercise in Southern humor-apologetics but is instead setting out to examine the presidency in light of (and to make light of) Carter's flagging popularity. The first of many country music lyrics (*Crackers* started out as a book about country music) implies the concession to defeat and Blount's ability to find a victory in art to offset the political defeat:

> I got the redneck White House blues.
> The man just makes me more and more confused.
> He's in all the right churches
> And all the wrong pews.
> I got the redneck White House blues. (13)

If the most explicit contrast in *Crackers* is between sections (actually between the South and the Nation), the most implicit is between the persona in the essays and the president. The analysis of Carter-as-Georgian continues to stress the president's failure—calculated or otherwise—to become the apotheosis of Southernness, which the humorist can be if he wants to (and not be also, of course). The humorist points out, without directly stating the contrast, that Jimmy Carter lacks the gift of language and quotability, a point first made in "Nyah." Although Blount rejects a feeler extended by a Carterite that he hire on as a presidential speech writer in a new "Crackro-American Camelot," the humorist does go so far as to imagine a future campaign song that would certainly be spurned by Carter:

> Let's have no more malaise, exacerbating,
> Tensions, finding fault and Cracker baiting,
> This tendency to *epater les cous rouges*
> Won't solve our problems, they are too huge.
> And, after all, he came from humble origins,
> And something you should know concerning Georgians . . . (19–20)

The "voice" interrupts, "*What!? What kind of damn campaign song?*"

The persona in Blount's essays is himself an outsider, enervated, not hotly engaged, one whose sympathies result in language and nothing else. If so, why is this analyst, even though he is a humorist, not dismissible as simply another cheap-shooting critic? Blount seeks to win the reader's confidence and forbearance by confessing his own failure. In "Yazoo," for instance, he recalls writing editorials for the *Atlanta Journal* and achieving a "measure of significance just by standing opposed to the forces of hate." For Blount, however, there is no fresh, heroic, political role, because "Southern liberalism had about been mapped out and settled" (21). The persona in Blount's humor puts himself in the same predicament Mark Twain created in "The Private History of a Campaign That Failed": after a war has been won, the humorist is on the safe side, a survivor but no hero, and covering with humor the treason of the writer. (In the opening of "Heterosexism and Dancing," Blount apologizes for studying literature at Vanderbilt in the early sixties "when I should have been desegregating luncheonettes." Later, when he writes of his army service during the Vietnam era, he implies that he was washed out of command school and assigned stateside desk work because he was not tough enough. In fact, there is no evidence that Blount avoided participation in either the civil rights movement or the Vietnam War, and his editorials and columns from Vanderbilt and the *Atlanta Journal* indicate no evasion and little in the way of modest self-effacement.) Uneasily liberal, uncomfortably Southern, writing from Massachusetts as Clemens had from Connecticut, elusive politically and evasive morally, Blount's persona tends to overassert and underretract, to comment boldly and then undercut mildly, remaining as ambivalent as Miss Lillian amongst the psychohistorians.

Although the humor reduces, the humor itself resists reduction; it remains so circular and circumspect that no literal, clear, and paraphrasable summary of the humorist's position is possible. The humorist is, in effect, outdoing Jimmy Carter in a deep parody, more than a superficial takeoff, that is at the heart of the humor.

How to preserve ambivalence is demonstrated when the humorist feints at analyzing the celebrated rabbit incident, in an essay appropriately entitled "The Damnedest Thing." Why did Carter tell anyone about using a boat paddle to fend off an attacking rabbit? Why did the president expose himself to conflicting accounts in news stories and to the sure-to-come condescending analyses by national political columnists such as Jack Germond and Jules Witcover? Why didn't Carter, like any other proper Southerner, brain the rabbit and be done with it? Blount evades in a manner that would do honor to any politician by assuming the posture of the apologetic, defensive Southerner facing an aggressive, offensive nation, represented by the media: "When you're a Cracker, you're always having something to disprove. *Everybody* in Western civilization has something to disprove, but not everybody realizes it. Everybody just realizes that the president is a Cracker who does not even have the propriety to be a mean one" (35).

In the process of apparently not knowing what to make of the president, the humorist observes carefully how Carter rose to power. His victory was over the region and the nation; he absorbed political rivals, trends, and the culture as he ascended; and though he failed to satisfy the image of the good old boy in any of its turns and inflections, he did rise as a nonsectional figure, a "Christopher Robin or David Copperfield or Charlie Brown or Pogo—a flat, bland, too-nice central figure, a good old cipher." Whatever the stereotype of Carter, the man had exhibited political genius:

He pointedly won without courting Mayor Daley or the Kennedys, although Jimmy had ridden a long way on his supposed resemblance to Jack. He diluted the influence of Senator Herman Talmadge, took over and neutralized the constituency of George Wallace, soaked up the legacy of Martin Luther King. He established the irrelevance of Hubert Humphrey. He deposed Henry Kissinger. (And his region caused the humiliation and shedding of Nelson Rockefeller.) Jimmy made capital out of Bob Dylan, the Allman Brothers, and the once-wonderful Cracker poet James Dickey *just* before it became generally apparent that they had shot their creative bolts. (73–74)

By the time *Crackers* was published in August 1980, Jimmy Carter's political fortunes were waning and Blount had a national consensus as a purchase for his humor. If Carter had failed to satisfy the nation that had sought an unambivalent, generic honest man, and the South had been disappointed that Carter was not a representative regional type, the entire country would do well to reexamine his brother, the exemplary redneck, good old boy, and alter ego of the humorist.

In two long essays, Blount presents portraits of Billy Carter, before and after the Libyan trouble. In the first, the humorist shows what he can make of his material—and how what he makes of it is more sympathetic, objective, and complete than accounts that accept and inevitably pass a negative judgment on the stereotype. In "Early Billy," Blount's first engagement with the Carter phenomenon, published in *Playboy* in 1977 and rewritten for *Crackers,* the humorist opens with third-person description before introducing himself as character and interviewer-for-the-nation. He shows Billy at the service station in Plains, trapped by a tourist and forced to pose with a can of beer: "Glumly, silently, with the air of a dog being dressed, Billy takes the beer and holds it up" (91). After describing the frenzy of Billy Carter, his family, and friends, under assault from the tourists, Blount approaches the issue of Billy Carter as a public figure, a celebrity with an agent, and a vicious humorist. In a Nashville bank lobby Billy tells a man who has been waiting in line to shake his hand, "That's quat a sports coat." When the man replies that he paid only fifteen dollars for it, Billy says, "You both got screwed" (96). Unlike the psychohistorians, Blount lets the surfaces speak and keeps his conclusions tentative. Though he has great fun dealing with the stereotype of Billy and translating his nature to a condescending and judgmental nation, Blount knows where to stop, where to briefly insert the serious:

It is true that Billy sleeps badly, smokes and drinks more than is healthy, shows a lot of aggression and has apparently been known to get a chip on his shoulder.

He may resent something. He may resent that people tend to assume that a man from South Georgia is quaint, for one thing. And he may resent that his father died when he was fourteen or that he is going to die himself sometime. In Nashville, the night of his fortieth birthday, a lady asked him what his greatest goal in life was and he said, "Ma'am, it's to live to be forty-one. And I think I'm over the hump." (101)

By 1979, Billy Carter had become less quaint; the comic redneck had given way to Sidey's "wily and greedy buffoon," and Blount had another side of the president's brother to study. In "Later Billy" Blount brushes past the pathos to attack the treatment of it and the media's refusal to allow to a Southerner the privileges granted to others outside the general American ethos. He argues that Billy Carter has been used by the media "the way stripminers use land" (121) and that Billy is being condemned because of his lack of pretense: "Here's a stark contrast in Southern communications: William Styron gets millions of dollars and critical esteem for writing page after page of presumptuously empathic bad prose about a concentration camp victim, and Billy Carter gets nothing but abuse for an authentic and not unrepresentative whiff of himself" (124). Blount's broadside against the world of publishing eventually lands him in his own Carter-like dilemma. Billy Carter is victimized by an "official morality in the media" that is "amendable, and also defensible, and in many ways elevating. But often cheap" (124). He does not have the license Muhammad Ali would have in comparing Arabs and Jews because "a certain leeway is allowed proved frank colorful black folk heroes whose temporal power is not great enough for their blind spots to be generally oppressive" (125). Blount looks at liberties accorded other ethnic groups and is rankled that Jews can criticize others but take offense at Billy's remarks. He continues the literary references by singling out Norman Podhoretz's condescending comments about good old boys, but he is reluctant to pursue any generalized criticism of Jews. He finds it refreshing that Norman Mailer, writing in the third person in *Armies of the Night*, would confess to a "curious, simple, and very unpleasant emotion" by admitting that "he was getting tired of Negroes and their rights." Asserting and qualifying, Blount says that "nobody has given this matter of Jews and the media the rigorous and mostly grateful consideration it deserves" (128), and he is not offended at David Steinberg's joke about being afraid of everything, including pork: "I'm afraid eating pork makes you stupid" (128). Blount's response to the Steinberg slur stretches his credibility, and his praise of the Jewish influence, even while stewing that the Southern joke (outdumbing instead of outsmarting the nation) cannot get equal play, sounds, at best, ingenuous, more like Jimmy than Billy Carter. The persona appears momentarily as a hat-in-hand supplicant, a Southerner too cautious about offending his own powerful literary and publishing constituency.

The final word on Billy Carter fortunately rings truer, and it also clarifies Blount's attitude toward the president's Southernness:

> The first Cracker President should have been a mixture of Jimmy and Billy, a cobbler of Billy's basic blackberries oozing up into and through Jimmy's cut-to-specifications crust. Billy's hoo-Lord-what-the-hell-get-out-of-the-way attitude heaving up under Jimmy's prudent self-righteousness—or Jimmy's idealism heaving up under Billy's sense of human limitations—and forming a nice-and-awful compound like life in Georgia, like life—I wouldn't be surprised—in other areas of the country that have not been over-mediaized. That Cracker President would have had a richer voice, and a less dismissable smile." (131–32)

What about that smile? No close observer of Jimmy Carter could avoid commenting on it. In a study of the president, it ranks as a charged and unavoidable consideration, with the moving of the part in his hair from right to left and the rabbit incident. Blount begins by saying he is inclined to defend Carter's grin "as the natural defense of a person who is trying to stay composed, and think, and not offend, and not really pander," but, after admitting that he never cared for Jimmy's smile himself, Blount sets off on an essay that winds up with him calling the expression "denatured," "troubling," and not the most honest "shit-eating grin" he's ever seen. Yet it is related more to the office of the president than to Carter's regional roots; it reflects the vicarious role of the chief executive, who must consume the defecation represented by history, economics, death, tradition, realism, exhaust, bad faith, and guilt for the country—"and maybe if anybody can do it, it's a Cracker." By the time of the Iran crisis, Blount notes, Carter's peculiar grin was gone and the "pressures of his office and his jogging and his sufferance of all those wild redneck Iranians had given him a truly hurt-looking austerity" (141).

Since *Crackers* does not purport to be logical or rational analysis (though, in fact, it is), the humorist can reach into the milieu as he pleases. Blount creates his humor with lateral transitions that link several controversial topics within a single essay, always returning eventually to Jimmy Carter and the South. For instance, in "Heterosexism and Dancing" the humorist moves from Allen Tate's remarks condemning homosexual poets, to understanding sexuality, to grotesqueries, to trying to tell the truth about what we do not understand. Blount is bold enough to introduce homosexuality and adrogyny, but he does not condemn them outright. Typically, he circles a position, looking less for a correct opinion than for a sensible attitude. He agrees and disagrees with Allen Tate; he is for and not for homosexuality; he is against androgyny, except metaphorically; and he finally finds his favorite, literary resolution: "I have always felt that homosexuals, like Southerners, are chosen people; it is our part to be out of whack, to hold back, to be unamalgamated" (216). In fact, the dogma in *Crackers,* as in much of Blount's writing, is limited to literature. He rises to high dudgeon against the North Carolina novelist Reynolds Price, who wrote "in a tedious celebratory piece" in the *Washington Post* on Carter's inauguration day that the idea of the Southerner's peculiarity "was spread by Northeastern journalists who had 'understandably stultified themselves on a diet of Faulkner and Flannery O'Connor (writers who some thoughtful Southerners see as sports to the region—homeless rhapsodists, fantasts, mesmerized haters).'" Blount identifies himself with such literary "sports"—a conception that informs all of Blount's writing—and again distances himself from such glib apologists as Price and Jimmy Carter, who, in an interview with Harvey Shapiro in the *New York Times Book Review,* had said, "I think in many ways now that those former dark moods in the South of recrimination against self and others and alienation from the rest of the nation—I think they've been alleviated." Blount identifies Carter's comments as the kind of rhetoric any boy raised in Atlanta during the 1950s would recognize, "Southern Chamber of Commerce Pride talking," and his response to the Carter who would say "alleviated" in that context is simply and appropriately, "*Shit,* Jimmy" (217).

Two essays placed near the end of the book indicate that Blount's basic points about Jimmy Carter have already been made. "Possumism," rewritten from the 1976 *Sports Illustrated* article, resembles the expository writing in *About Three Bricks Shy of a Load.* Carter's tangent barely touches the circle of this long account of possums, possum showing, and possum eating; Blount concludes that the possum is harder to know but is "more simple" than Jimmy is. The essay entitled "Jrs." is a Blount tour de force, a real psychological insight followed by a catalog of famous juniors, a literary exploration, and some legitimate wonder about the impact of being one: "Father-son unity confuses roles. Hamlet (like Jimmy Carter) is an ill-focused Jr. in a post-assassination time. The new king, murderer of Hamlet, Sr., has usurped not only Hamlet's mother and patrimony but also Hamlet's Oedipal right to kill his own father—something Jrs. are more than normally

ambivalent about to begin with" (251). In the mystery that is Jimmy
Carter, Blount touches on a troubling national-familial relationship:
"You don't resent President Carter the way a child resents a parent,
but the other way around" (255). In "Approaching the White House,"
Blount deepens the tone by comparing Jimmy Carter with another
Georgian and junior, Martin Luther King, whom Blount had seen and
whose funeral he had attended. But he finds Carter lacking the ability
of King—and Nixon and Lester Maddox—to "cut into the fundamen-
tum." Carter never rose to large paternal heights; and Blount implies
that the devices of the traditional humorist—ridicule, satire, pleasant
jokes even—in making fun of a character of such middling stature have
produced no great yield. His analysis of that riddle is profound: "You
want to lay into him. But when you do, you feel like you're picking
on someone smaller and more earnest than your image of your*self*"
(283). The last essay includes a review of the 1980 candidates and a
brief eulogy for an administration that has suffered "the curse of Georgians." Carter's departure leaves Blount "an American" with "some
poignance to my ethnos" (290). Lest the book be taken as profound or
sentimental or the author himself claim the last word, Blount gives it
instead to "Dogsbody Carter," never one to curry favor, who could call
anybody who described him as likable "a dumb son of a bitch."

Without a doubt *Crackers* made a direct hit, on the president and
with the nation. *Washington Post* reporter Ed Walsh, writing the press
pool report for the president's trip from Beaumont to Waco, Texas, on
22 October 1980, said that Carter's press secretary, Jody Powell, "de-
manded" that acerbic ABC correspondent Sam Donaldson give a dramatic rendering of "the mean and slashing attack on a dynamic duo of
Washington political columnists" [Jack Germond and Jules Wit-
cover].[8] Presidential speech writer Rick Hertzberg wrote Blount that
even the president was influenced by the book: "I'm convinced that
J.C. would never have started talking about horse manure at all if it
hadn't been for 'Crackers.' It's almost as if Jimmy decided to put a
little Billy in there, just like you recommended." Hertzberg and Powell exchanged readings of favorite passages, and Hertzberg noticed
three copies on the press plane, "two of which had lots of paper stuck
into them to mark different passages."[9]

In the flood of reviews, almost all favorable, Blount was compared,
variously, with Mark Twain, Ring Lardner, Bruce Jay Friedman, Richard Pryor, Philip Roth, and, of all people, Zero Mostel. In the regular

run of the *New York Times,* Anatole Broyard credited Blount with "the finest ear for Southern speech" since Mostel, in the role of Southern senator, had said, "Ah come from a state where there *are* no conditions."[10] Charles Simmons, an editor of the *New York Times Book Review,* confessed that he could not read from *Crackers* without "breaking up," and he delivered himself of advertising copy in the first sentence by comparing the book to *Portnoy's Complaint* and calling it "a comic masterpiece of ethnic ambivalence." Allowing that "Mr. Blount hisself is not a Cracker," Simmons pointed out that although the humorist went to Vanderbilt and Harvard, "he has a Cracker voice inside him."[11] In a long, laudatory review in the *Washington Post Bookworld,* Georgian and novelist Harry Crews called Blount's performance "a triumph over substance" and said that he "could not ask for a more knowledgeable, well-written commentary on our times."[12] In the *National Review,* Charles Culhane agreed with the dust-jacket blurb of William F. Buckley (another Jr.) that Blount is "a major humorist."[13] *Booklist* noted that "what seems achingly funny and irreverent on the surface is really serious and poignant commentary," and *Publishers Weekly* concluded, "Shrewd as it is ribald, the material on Billy Carter makes howlingly clear why Blount prefers him, a redneck original, over the brother who lost his birthright in D.C."[14]

Reviewers who were less amused also recognized the ambivalence toward the president and the South but interpreted Blount's position as adamantly pro-South and anti-Carter. Donald Morrison, reviewing for *Time,* found *Crackers* "a cunning, amusing and not always pertinent decoupage of articles centering on Blount's South pole," with an "overarching thesis" that "contemporary America, like its President, is too emotionally constrained, too given to artifice, too Northern."[15] Gene Lyons in the *Nation* called *Crackers* "a shamelessly patched together series of magazine articles, little more than a sustained hooraw written to get even with the prigs who don't understand the South." He saw the book as being built around one basic joke: "Southerners who seem dumb are really fully of sly wisdom." He concluded that Blount's efforts to justify his material on a thematic basis were "simply ludicrous" and that his "moments of wit . . . are a magazine writer's moments at best and do not justify the price of a hardback book."[16] In what is probably the only academic journal review of *Crackers,* the book is granted two paragraphs in a ringingly self-righteous, allusion-laden, six-book sweep by Spencer Brown in the *Sewanee Review,* in which the humorist is dismissed as "a poor man's Lenny Bruce, a poor-mouth tedium devoted to hatred of Jimmy Carter." Brown found Blount "fascinated by micturition, defecation, and (a rare adult touch) copulation."[17]

Even though a minority may have been micturating and moaning, Roy Blount, Jr., had succeeded in addressing a national audience and humoring it with writings about the South, by a Southerner. His humor provided a fresh, intelligent, and informed perspective on Carter and national politics, and it encouraged reviewers to recruit for Blount. The *Washington Monthly* blurb flowed with the enthusiasm of the general reader:

> Even if you never want to read another *word* about Billy . . . or anyone else name of Carter . . . don't let that keep you away from *Crackers*. Whatever it is you're doing that seems so terribly important, put it down and go get yourself a copy of this book and about nine cold cans of Pearl beer and all your old Chuck Berry records, and send the kids off to play with their friends so you can sit somewhere comfortable and laugh out loud without feeling self-conscious. Be grateful to the South for producing writers like Roy Blount, and promise yourself not to feel guilty if you never read another word on the op-ed page of the *Times*.[18]

By the end of *Crackers*, Roy Blount had exhausted Jimmy Carter: he had looked at the man, the presidency, and the nation and had defined Carter by showing what he was not. Finally, Blount, in his way, "strip-mined" Jimmy Carter, without using him up. He acknowledged that the mystery of Jimmy Carter was not resolved, and he returned the president to Georgia, gently, just before the electorate did.

Crackers is the humorist's victory over the politician and the nation. Winning on his own subtle terms, Blount claims for himself the national audience that his fellow Southerner lost. In the competition, he supplants the politician, gaining both a national constituency and the national favor. (In fact, in comparing the Carter brothers, he implies that the president failed because he was not humorist enough.) Although Ronald Reagan never presented Blount with such rich, complicated, and personal material, the idea of the humorist as president has continued to inform Blount's writing. Without a nod to Pat Paulsen, the comedian with the deadpan face who made the routine popular in the 1960s, Blount has continued to create humor by equating the president and the humorist. When a conservative president with a prominent cold streak and no regional identification took on more power than Jimmy Carter ever had, Blount's circuitousness moved toward audacity and his queasiness toward muffled outrage. After demonstrating in *Crackers* that humor can be a tool for sympathetic political analysis, Blount faced an unambivalent presidency that inspired satire.

Chapter Six
A National Humorist: The Four Collections

> And I love collections! I even love to read the page, up front, that
> tells where the various pieces first appeared (see up front). I got a
> whole level further into a person once because of how eagerly she
> crouched by the anthology shelf at the Gotham Book Mart. What
> kind of fool am I? Miscellaneous.
> —Roy Blount, Jr., "On Miscellaneity: Juice Swapping," in *One
> Fell Soup* (1984)

Crackers, contends Roy Blount, Jr., in the first essay of his first anthology, is not a collection, despite what some reviewers said. Although the thematic ordering around President Carter and the South
does distinguish *Crackers* from the four, less unified collections that
follow, the 1980 book is the first indication of Blount's skill in shaping
free-lance writing into a single work and of his ability to create for the
writing and for himself a new context. In the movement from magazine to book contexts, cosmetic but significant shifts in genre take
place: "articles" become "essays," "doggerel" may be called "light
verse," and a mere journalist is transmogrified into an anthologist. The
collections after *Crackers* indicate that Blount and the publishers considered his humor to be a body of work, more than ephemeral journalism and worthy of being republished in books that would widen his
popularity and earn him critical attention.

The collections have never been Blount's principal source of income.
Even by the time *Crackers* was published, he was a self-sustaining free-
lance magazine writer. Apparently Blount's books have sold well, if
remaining in print is a valid standard for judging success. (In 1989,
all of them, except *It Grows on You,* were in print. *Crackers* was scheduled for a new Ballantine edition, and *About Three Bricks Shy of a Load*
was being republished, with new material and an addition to the title,
"and the Load Filled Up.") None of the collections made the best-seller
lists, but they increased Blount's popularity, hence both the demand

and the fees for free-lance work and public appearances. The four major collections (excluding *It Grows on You,* which is really one long essay, with photographs, and *Soupsongs/Webster's Ark,* which is solely light verse) proved that the sum of Blount's work exceeds the parts, and, moreover, they concentrated the humor so that reviewers for national magazines and prominent newspapers could see his writing as more than occasional magazine articles, often done on assignment, some of them as regular column work.

Without the collections, Blount probably would not be regarded as a literary humorist at all, because the persona of Roy Blount, Jr., the literary humorist, emerges only in the anthologies. In his books, the persona appears as a fully independent presence, rather than as subordinate to a football team, a president or a magazine. The persona comes together in the physical body of a book, revealing a sensibility capable of speaking to, and for, a generation, a social class, and a moment in time.

As central events in Blount's literary career, the book publications have distanced him from the periodicals, from his peers in magazine journalism, and from the social and political issues he has treated within the separate publications. The collections have also amplified and unified his magazine work, broadened his audience, and required that he find currents within his own thought for organizing the anthologies. Taken together, the four major collections open a window onto the transformation of Blount into a nationally known humorist, with one eye on the shifting times and the other on the verities, literary and otherwise.

One Fell Soup, or I'm Just a Bug on the Windshield of Life

Both the title and the subtitle of the first collection are purely and strangely Blount. ("I'm Just a Bug on the Windshield of Life" is a song title in the "Whiskey and Blood" essay in *Crackers.*) The fifty-eight collected pieces draw on his entire writing career; in *One Fell Soup* (1982) he resurrected and reshaped writings from high school and the *Atlanta Journal,* fitting into the collections earlier pieces with more recent magazine articles and reaching for a main title to embrace them. The punning title from *Macbeth* suggests *salmagundi,* first used by Washington and William Irving and James Kirke Paulding to apply a gustatory metaphor to an American literary miscellany.

Handy, general, and often mutually inclusive, the six main groupings within *One Fell Soup*—"Issues and Answers," "Animal and Vegetable Spirits," "Used Words," "Love and Other Indelicacies," "Sports Afield," and "Wired into Now"—define Blount's range as closet editorialist, eccentric gourmet, wordsmith, sex commentator, sportswriter, and culture critic. Though in the later collections the divisions have titles more clever and figurative, they are synonyms for the subject-matter headings in *One Fell Soup,* which stake out a territory large enough to admit almost any academic, social, or political topic; as a whole, they signify that Blount is more than a sportswriter or a stage Southerner.

The polemical voices, regional and national, juxtaposed in *Crackers* do not generate the humor in *One Fell Soup* or, for that matter, in any of the other three major collections. Rather than opposing the neutral, third-person voice and the vernacular first person, as he had learned to do at *Sports Illustrated* before perfecting the routine in *Crackers,* Blount uses a primary voice, that of the persona, together with the voices of several subpersonae. The dominant voice in *One Fell Soup* is that of the editorial-columnist-turned-humorist, freed of the restrictions of writing to a general newspaper audience, relieved of the main burden of writing expository prose, and given the moral and editorial liberty to speak directly to enlightened equals, with no obvious restraints except the author's. The secondary voices, whether they are singing a song to okra or preaching a parody of Scientific Creationist evangelism, channel the persona through speakers addressing the same readers, whom the writing assumes to be capable of snapping up allusions to literature, history, philosophy, sports, science, and schlock journalism.

The failure to satisfy the notion of what a tightly organized collection should be bothered at least two *One Fell Soup* reviewers, the more outspoken of which was a Boston librarian. Reviewing for *Library Journal,* A. J. Anderson said Blount's individual *"patisseries"* had "momentary appeal" but that the pieces "en masse . . . resemble nothing so much as an assortment of immiscible ingredients. Indeed, his ceaselessly wild and wooly puns and japeries begin after a while to cloy. It's simply too much jabberwocky to take straight." The librarian finished off *One Fell Soup* in one foul word: "Dispensable."[1] Reviewers who were more likely to read the entire collection at a sitting would also be more likely to read for textual unity or consistency, but even so, most of those reviewing *One Fell Soup* liked the pacing. Christopher Lehmann-Haupt in the *New York Times* said an "extraordinarily high percentage" of the pieces managed "to hit the mark," and Cathleen Shine in the *Nation,* while finding a few "dead spots," said that "the book saunters by, humming merrily" and that "Blount investigates the homeliest phenomena with such burning thoroughness that the pieces become implicit parodies of every solemn, semischolarly academic or journalistic inquiry."[2]

The essays in *One Fell Soup* first appeared in *Esquire, Playboy, Organic Gardening,* and eighteen other publications that Blount describes in his introduction as "almost pathologically disparate." Blount does not comment directly on any of the periodicals, not even the *New Yorker,* which had rejected the humor written during his army days. Where the pieces initially appeared is not considered critically significant, even though in some of the essays the persona refers to himself as "this column." Although there are five italicized afternotes updating or clarifying details, the context of the collection contributes to the impression that the pieces are being read for the first time (and they apparently were by most of the reviewers). Some of the pieces are old—ancient—by the standards of newspaper journalism; however, those Blount winnowed from his magazine writings were fresh or universal enough in subject, style, and sensibility to be relevant to the 1982 readers of *One Fell Soup.*

Indeed, among the essays in the first collection are some of Blount's universal best: "The Singing Impaired" (now a Blount trademark), "The Socks Problem," "Chickens," "The New Writing Aids," "The Times: No Sh*t," "The Orgasm: A Reappraisal," "The Family Jewels," "Jock Lingerie," "The Presidential Sports Profile," "Why There Will Never Be a Great Bowling Novel," and "Facing Ismism." Except for the topical references to Carter, Reagan, and John Anderson (the last a soon-to-be-forgotten independent candidate for president in 1980) and the description of Jim Palmer in the Jockey underwear advertisement, these essays are not dated, and even the idea in the presidential sports profile cries out for quadrennial reapplication.

Blount's literary techniques come from the personal essay and from prose fiction. A topic is "essayed," or tried, turned slowly from a variety of perspectives suggested by the topic as it strikes the sensibility of the persona, or whatever subpersonae the humorist might assume. As the humor gravitates from the essay to the fictional sketch, perspective becomes point of view, usually first person but occasionally omniscient. In the *Crackers* caricatures and in the "blue yodels" of *What Men Don't Tell Women,* Blount uses multiple voices that speak in various vernaculars, in dialogue that is in descant to the straighter voice of the dominant persona. In *One Fell Soup*, Blount does not organize the text around this contrapuntal structure; nevertheless, the voice of the writer or persona—though it is wild aplenty at times, never stuffy and never dull—remains unmistakably the center from which the other voices or characters radiate. Essentially the same persona Blount used in *Crackers*, it is marked by the paradoxes of coolness and passion, amusement and irritation, and irreverence and rectitude.

How these contrasts create humor is best demonstrated in Blount's essay on testicles. "The Family Jewels," first published in *Playboy* in March 1982, is a five-thousand-word mock-treatise, written without prurience or prudery and with a frank, comically calm circumspection. Blount shows how perceptions of testicles depend on sexual role changes, male bluster, general insecurities, exact anatomical descriptions, etymological ironies, food, sports, tall tales, and American literature. Though by 1982 the sexual slang Blount uses was common in movies and on pay television, there was shock value left in the printed expression of it. Moving the slang from the context of *Playboy* to that of *One Fell Soup* also heightened the shock potential. Even more perilous than using the words themselves (which still might keep the book off some school and public library shelves) is Blount's abrupt but, at the same time, balanced descriptions of sexual politics:

Woman has been known to keep man down by self-fulfilling disparagement of his masculinity. Man has been known to batter woman and then to expect her not to damage his fragile ego (down there below the rugae [which Blount has defined as skin folds of the scrotum]) by telling anybody. A man who abuses women often justifies himself by calling them "ballbreakers." A woman who takes pleasure in kicking men in the crotch, literally or figuratively, often justifies herself by calling them insensitive to any other kind of feeling. There is a real sense in which women have men by the balls, and there are real grounds for a cultural imperative against women's taking that advantage. But there is also a sense in which men have women by the lack of balls. Freud said that the female equivalent of the male fear of castration is fear of the loss of love. Maybe, if enough women wear Charlie perfume and get gold American Express cards, that will change. (146–47)

The one paragraph is a paradigm of the style of Blount's persona in the role of general literary humorist. Dealing with a topic about which males are likely to be uneasy and curious and to which coarse reference is common, he does not stop at the superficial. The real dramatic conflict is between men and women, and Blount centers his humor on what lies between them: violence, jealousy, false images—not simply testicles. Moving from the singular noun at the opening of the paragraph to the collective at the end, and from primitive to modern connotations, Blount separates the general offenses from the particular individuals who might take offense. (Which is not to say that a man or a woman, reading Blount, might associate the writer with either side and be offended.) When Blount's persona gets into the debate, he takes the romantic high ground: the worse part of the war between the sexes is the loss of love, brought on when the sexes cannot agree on roles; that sexual battle is joined when sexual roles transgress, and it is made absurd when the roles coalesce in one sex. But the burden of the humor does not rest on such a heavily moral and sentimental point.

Sexual conflict, necessarily suggested to the persona by testicles (which to another sensibility, could, as easily, necessarily suggest reconciliation), is less important than the subject, which is inherently energetic and volatile, interesting enough to attract the curious but likely to lapse into cheap jokes and trivial observations. Whereas readers of *Playboy* might not respond to the idea of testicles as agents of procreation, that fact contributes to the subject's propriety and makes it controllable. Emphasis is placed on the relationship of testicles to male identity rather than to sexual pleasure. Exposition of the subject is the basis for the essay, and through exposition the persona can insert the humor. In trying the subject, the essayist can impart information and draw insights, not all of them straight, from the subject. For instance, writer and reader learn the following:

- *"Testis,* the singular, is Latin for 'witness,'" although Blount does not find in classical antiquity such a phrase as *"per cumulum testimum juro,"* which he translates as "I swear on a stack of testicles" (140).

- "[O]*rchid* is Greek for 'testicle,' which may account for the pride with which girls used to wear them on prom dresses, sometimes called 'ball gowns.' . . . The average human testis weighs one ounce. . . . A sperm whale's runs around fifty pounds apiece" (141).

- "Achilles' mother made him 99 percent immortal by holding him by the heel and dipping him into the river Styx. Mother Nature makes the average Joe 99 percent tough by holding on to his 'nads" (143).

- "The reason males get sterile if mumps 'go down' into the balls is that this outer layer, the *tunica albuginea,* is so inflexible that when the inner ball swells against it, the tubules are damaged. Ovaries, on the other hand, can expand and ride the mumps out" (145).

- "So perhaps it is not surprising that throughout most of American literature, balls have been conspicuous, if at all, by their absence. You have to read *The Sun Also Rises* carefully to gather that Jake Barnes has had his shot off in the war" (150).

Preceding "The Family Jewels" in the collection is "The Orgasm: A Reappraisal," its complement in several ways. Published first in *Cosmopolitan* in 1978, it was rejected, Blount adds in an afternote, by several men's magazines (137). A reader of *One Fell Soup* is left to his own conclusions as to why a men's magazine would publish a long, fact-filled essay on testicles and a women's magazine would accept a piece one-fifth as long spoofing serious studies of a trendy, late-seventies subject. Each of the pieces is laden with puns; Blount apologizes for ending his essay on testicles "dangling on such a low double entendre."

"The Orgasm: A Reappraisal" in *Cosmopolitan* is a parody of sociological and etymological profundities in which two "experts"—one of them a Wisconsin erotophysicist who has written a book entitled *But My Head Is Bending Low*—challenge "the orgasm's inviolate status." The first contends that orgasms are not ideal for everyone, because they are "loud, violent, and hard to govern"; are interfered with by lack of proper communication ("'Quick, quick, quick!' or 'Quit, quit, quit'"); and limit production: "Almost *no work* was done by Americans last year in the twenty minutes following orgasm—excepting those achieved after 12:45 P.M. on weekdays in massage parlors" (134). The second expert, a professor emeritus of classics from DesPond Junior College, Alabama, points out that the word *orgasm* derives from *Orgasmos,* "the Greek god of playing with dynamite, who lived way off back in a deep cave and only emerged to rain bad trouble and cold sores upon whoever had stirred him up"(135). The professor is disturbed that, since Americans have stopped studying Greek in high school, such poets as Personica Bumpers have treated "orgasm as romp"; her poem opens:

> *Orgasm, orgasm,*
> *Right up my chasm;*
> *Orgasm, orgasm,*
> *Undo my not!*
> *I want to have a lot!*

Again, Blount uses a double entendre for a deliberately anticlimactic closing: "Anti-Excitement Leagues are already being formed on college campuses, and there is even talk of going further, all the way to the downplaying of muscular contractions. As the saying goes, there is no delaying an idea whose time has . . . arrived" (137).

As voices and subjects vary, so does the implied reader. Most of Blount's essays reflect the general readers of the magazines, but occasionally he is speaking directly to writers. In fact, if anything is straight or serious in Blount it is his high regard for the art of writing and the act of reading. In a piece first published in *More* ("Is the Pope Capitalized?"), Blount reviews the Associated Press, United Press International, *New York Times,* and *Washington Post* stylebooks. He recognizes style, but, more the seasoned journalist than the humorist in this setting, he does not get entangled in definitions or descriptions of it. He points to the contexts in which various styles work, in particular the conventions of straight newswriting and personal-column writing, and he calls *style* "presence, or, as Swift said, 'proper words in proper places'" (81). As one who has edited and written in the forms he discusses, Blount relates this largest matter of style to the smallest, to capitalization, punctuation, and spelling options, and he shows how one writer reacts to the matter of style: "Personally, I resent the various stylebooks I have labored under, which have caused my *Okay* to become *O.K.,* my *grey* to become *gray,* my *barefooted* to go *barefoot.* Maybe such things don't bother you, but they make me feel messed with" (81). He scolds the *Post* for violating its own style in capitalizing *president,* and he chides the editor, Ben Bradlee, not for pointing out that *refused* and *admit* are pejorative but for failing to say "how they are loaded and how they might be unloaded" (83). On the question of sexism Blount agrees with all four stylebooks that "women should no longer be referred to gratuitously as mothers, wives, grandmothers, or objects of desire, as though the reporter felt obliged subtly and indirectly to imply an erection somewhere along the line every time a member of the female sex is mentioned," but as neither a purist nor a sexist (of either variety) Blount comes out for "bias openly arrived at, as in Dr. Johnson's dictionary" and in favor of the United Press International stylebook because "it reads like *some particular person* styled it to suit himorherself" (86–87).

In "The *Times*: No Sh*t," published first in the now-defunct *Soho News,* Blount finds it unfair that, given the presence of the word everywhere, a writer who is "expected to be mightier, day in and day out, than the sword" is reduced to saying *"stuff* or, just maybe, *excreta,"* when his interview quotes are printed in the *New York Times* (127). Blount sides, as he did in *Crackers,* with Norman Mailer, who told Lillian Ross that he would not write for the *New Yorker,* because the editors would not let him use the word. From his daughter, Blount learned a solution to the problem of propriety: never use an obscene word in front of people unless they have used it first. (Blount's afternote says a reader sent him a clipping showing that the *Times* had used the word first, in a direct quote.)

The issue of obscenity in Blount's prose style is, of course, larger than the essay on the *Times'* proscription indicates. In the anthologies the obscene word provides a necessary seasoning, a bold indication that Blount is not playing to the whole house and is not interested in coming across as droll and whimsical. "I always wanted to be coarse," Blount said, in an interview. "Too many American humorists have failed in the direction of primness, narrowness, the inability to say *shit."* In humor such as Blount's, which is founded on reason—the faculty used to recognize, classify, and comment on incongruities—the obscenity introduces both passion and earthiness. In the context of Blount's humor, it also shocks. To Blount, the writing of E. B. White has an "ethereal," otherworldly quality, and that of Thurber and even Lardner is marked by a prudishness, "a fear of pussy." Blount acknowledged the influence of the Old Southwest humorists, who juxtaposed a refined narrator against a raw central character, and of Richard Pryor, whose salty street talk is set in the context of his sense of suffering or the "blues"—a sense missing in the routines of Eddie Murphy, which makes Murphy's obscenity unjustifiable and offensive. "I never want to be polite or overly fastidious," Blount said. "I want to be elegant and rambunctious."[3]

In general, Blount's style, while it would never be mistaken for Andy Rooney's, does not depend on obscene language. Coarser words are confined to essays in *Playboy* and *Esquire* and to those written for the collections and are closely circumscribed by context. Obscene language is offset within each essay by the ironic attitude of the persona toward it or by the dramatization of it; essays that use the franker terms are also balanced within the context of the entire collection by essays that show the influence of the more fastidious humorists. Rambunctious enough not be trusted entirely, Blount never uses obscenity or any other language capriciously. "Chickens" and "That Dog Isn't Fifteen," for instance, are tightly controlled sketches suitable for reading to general audiences. The first is really a series of sketches, with an internal anecdote of childhood written in the Thurber mode, that Blount reads on one of the commercially available audiotapes, and the second, a dialogue between women involving the elopement of a relative with a television set, is the only story with two voices in *One Fell Soup.* "That Dog Isn't Fifteen" is sometimes read by Blount in his public appearances, though he has occasionally been unable to re-create both voices in an oral presentation.[4]

"Five Ives Gets Named," one side of a telephone conversation between a rookie baseball player and his brother back home, is obviously influenced by Ring Lardner's *You Know Me, Al,* an epistolary novel, but it is not a parody. Although it is a dramatic monologue, it is not so dependent upon dramatic irony, and the humor is not as black as Lardner's. Slipped five milligrams of an upper just before his first game in the majors, against "Tommy Damn John" in Yankee Stadium, the rookie tells of hitting a two-strike pitch for a home run:

Jim, I took Tommy John out of Yankee Stadium at the three-eighty-five in right center. Two men on, we're only behind one run for some reason, and WOOOM I put us ahead. I'm circling the damn Yankee bases, and you know, on the postgame shows they always ask 'em, "What were you thinking about, rounding the bases"? I'm thinking, "FIVE MILLIGRAMS!"

And I cross the plate and Boom Holmes gives me a high-five—Boom Holmes gives me one, Jim—which, a *high*-five, is appropriate as shit. And he says, "I didn't know you was that *strawng.*"

And all I can think to do, now everybody's slapping at me, is open my mouth and holler, "FIVE! FIVE!" (175)

The climax of the story is not the earning of the nickname but the full reaction to a home run hit while under the influence of more than the majors: "Hey Jim, don't, you know, don't tell Pop" (176). The manic bantering in "Five Ives" does not quite cover the anxiety. The story, first published in *Esquire* in 1982, shortly before this collection appeared, implies that drugs have lost their humorous appeal; there is too much pathos in the character's final comment for the ending to be funny.

In his introduction to *One Fell Soup,* Blount comments on the number of "persons" or "tracks" in the humor. The multiplicity indicates both the range of Blount's humor and magazine editors' recognition of that range. As his interests shifted away from many subjects and forms,

however, he began to concentrate on certain subjects and certain periodicals. Never abandoning his past, he began to alter the voice of his
persona, toning it down and turning it on a topic certain to find the
widest spectrum of readers.

What Men Don't Tell Women

Roy Blount's second collection is his first book to consist wholly of
humor pieces; hewing closer to a thematic line than *Crackers, What
Men Don't Tell Women* (1984) is less random in its ordering than *One
Fell Soup* and is addressed to an audience exercised over the most per-
vasive social question of the day. Many of the pieces were published in
leading magazines, but they appear written to serve the book rather
than, as in *One Fell Soup,* the other way round. Unlike *Crackers,* the
second collection has no poetry and little in the way of exposition, and
it includes only residues of the earliest work. The increased stylistic
flexibility, the even-narrower literary allusions, and the slipping away
of restraints on explicit sexual diction help create a fresher, more confident, less inhibited book of humor, indicating that Blount had found
himself and his audience and was capable of taking greater risks. In
the process of nationalizing his humor Blount was moving away from
the sportswriter-journalist persona and closer to that of domestic
spokesman and public performer in a nettlesome time—in short, closer
to Benchley. He was addressing Benchley's class of readers, and he was
angling directly for their social and sexual anxieties, less to state answers than, like Benchley, to act out answers for them.

The uniformity of focus and tone in *What Men Don't Tell Women* is
traceable to the magazines for which the major essays were written, to
the short span in which they were written, and to the relationship-
between-the-sexes question Blount centers on. Of the twenty-five main
essays, nine first appeared in the *Atlantic* (two cannibalized from ideas
in the *Atlanta Journal* columns), three in *Esquire* (perhaps the best essay
in the collection, "Women in the Locker Room!," was written for *Esquire* but rejected during a management change), two in *Gentleman's
Quarterly,* two in *Playboy,* and one each in *Vanity Fair, Vogue, Los Angeles
Herald Examiner,* the *New York Times Book Review, Outside,* the *TWA
Ambassador, Madison Avenue,* and the *HCA* [Hospital Corporation of
America] *Companion.* The introduction draws on an interview with the
editors of *Ladies' Home Journal.* These magazines represent a class of
readers, unified socially and economically—most of them middle-

aged, well read, probably liberal, monied, acquisitive, eastern, sub-urban, white—and bifurcated by gender-specific magazines. Blount's range easily embraces such a readership and finds enough latitude within it to create variety. The varying editorial guidelines allow for movement from the uninhibited language of *Playboy* to the straiter lacing of the *Atlantic,* from the *New York Times Book Review* to the TWA in-flight magazine, and from *Vogue* to *Gentleman's Quarterly.* Within this class of readers are two mind-sets—contemporary women and men, feminism and machoism—each needful of support and gentle correction.

To hold the principal issue before the readers and to keep the collection from appearing amorphous, Blount wrote new interchapters, called "blue yodels," after the country-blues songs of Jimmie Rodgers (also, the sometimes racist and sexist characters in these sketches use bluer language). Shorter than the main essays and set in italics, these twenty-seven monologues, skits, and sketches give the reader a rest from the main persona and present, consistently, a male point of view. The "blue yodelers" talk about women, often in passionately sexist ways, and, in talking, generally expose themselves as selfish and un-heroic but not really despicable. As a literary distancing device, the blue yodels allow for a franker exploration of the consequences of male-female role changes than the humorist dared risk using the voice of his persona. In the introduction, Blount said, "I decided to prize apart the book's intricately interlocking pieces and insert certain scraps of testimony, from men of many stripes, revealing for the first time the things men don't tell" (7–8). These interchapters also increase the fun and the fictive quality, and they provide a frame for individual essays and for the entire book.

Blount opens and closes the book with a blue yodel monologue by Joseph—except for one dialogue, the speakers are male, with first names only—who describes a "Men and Masculinity" workshop at which he has been urged by Rose (never identified as a wife, though as domineering as Maggie or Maude), who has completed her asser-tiveness training and who, Joseph tells his buddies, *"said if she was going to continue relating to me in a broader sense I needed to go through tenderness training and claim my wholeness"* (11). At the end of the book, Rose has sent Joseph to a "Male Empowerment" workshop because in the course of sensitizing himself he has become "too androgynous," suppressing a "natural male energy"; expressing that energy once was irritating and now "suppressing it pisses women off" (187). The changes Joseph goes through in trying not only to please Rose but also to stay up with the social trends are repeated in several other interchapters and in most of the essays.

In spirit, most of the blue yodel males are Joseph's brothers. Black or white, Southern or Northern, Jewish or Italian, they are reactionaries, put on the defensive, uncomfortable in expressing their maleness (*manhood* would be as offensive as *machismo*), and tyrannized by private and public perceptions of their gender. They are victims of the times, actually of the national will, reflected in the sensibilities of the publications in which Blount's essays appear, but they are mostly deserving victims. Though he feints at the role, Blount never becomes the curmudgeon, taking up for henpecked men who, metamorphosed into yuppie Prufrocks, do not deserve defense. But not all his men fit the comic-strip/sit-com molds, and the sympathy they engender is subtler, more literary, and funnier. They are in a comic but many-layered bind.

The women in Blount's writings, most often depicted indirectly through male eyes, are consistently less aware that they are also victims, not of men but of having won the debate over what constitutes manners at society's leading edge. In one of the funniest sketches, a husband named Cooper describes the problem in expressing fidelity to women:

> *Or maybe you say you are faithful and here's how they go. They get rigid. Get struck to the core. And they say, "Who is she?"*
>
> *Right? and you say—you're astounded. You say: "No, I didn't say anything about infidelity. I said fidelity. Fih. Fih." That's a bad thing about that word. You feel silly saying "Fih."*
>
> *And they say, "Is she pretty?"*
>
> *And you say, "No!" And then you're dead.* (176)

Struggling for a generalizing metaphor to explain the basic differences between the sexes and growing progressively confused, Cooper comes up with this: "*Women are people who live on this gossamer plane full of blood, and then when they think you've torn it, they have these steel teeth*" (176). Cooper is as verbally whipped as Harry, who says, "*You know, a woman can take something you said and repeat it back to you in this tone of voice like it's obviously exactly the kind of statement Adolf Hitler always made*" (81). Like Joseph and Cooper, Marv also feels role-shift anxiety. He tells his buddy: "*I talked to April's psychiatrist. He explained that she felt overpowered by me because I was so objective. I should lose my temper, he said. I talked to*

*April about it. She said he was right. So the next time she cried, I yelled and
flung my arms and jumped up and down and got incoherent. It did me a lot
of good. You know what she said. 'I thought I could at least count on you to
be objective'"* (132).

What men don't tell women is that the old masculine support system is rickety and that, if there was a war, women have already won
it. Men are at the mercy of women, though they will not say it, and
if they did, women would passionately disagree and win the argument.
What women don't tell men, Blount's humor implies, is that women
are not comfortable being thought of as victors. Yet there is no reconciliation, compromise, or closure throughout the progress of the
blue yodels. Because Blount's criticisms of trend-driven women are
directed through men too insecure or myopic to engender much sympathy, the persona remains well out of the line of fire. A solution, a
position, or even a direct comment would break the tone and destroy
the humor. Nevertheless, the tension is real and deep, and, the
sketches suggest, will not be laughed away. Joseph and Rose, in the
world without end of this humor, will continue reversing roles, and
hapless Joseph, reluctantly doing Rose's bidding, will, of course, fail
to satisfy her or himself.

The longer essays in *What Men Don't Tell Women* are less personal,
though many turn on the issue of sexual roles. In "Why Wayne Newton's Is Bigger than Yours," which treats money and the size of salaries
and was first published in February 1983 as a *Playboy* article, Blount
draws on childhood and adult experiences and on his wide readings in
psychology and economics. He has a particular bit of fun pursuing to
its logical and modern end Freud's equating a baby's feces with an
adult's money:

Then the parents start teaching the baby to save it. He's been enjoying it,
using it to bring loved ones to his bedside, playing mud pie with it when he's
bored. Now they want him to hold it in until he can deposit it into a shiny,
impersonal facility very like a bank. Everybody is proud of him when he does
this, and then—*floosh!*—the stuff is gone. And the part of him that produced
it gets covered back up, along with other things, by his pants (which in due
time will have, in the rear, a wallet pocket). (100–1)

Looking at the discrepancies in salaries—Wayne Newton's making
$5,769.23 an hour and "the average general-duty nurse $5.93"—
Blount follows the trial of the subject to a tentative conclusion that

one reason for women making an average of $131 a week less than men "is that women—for whatever tangled reasons of tradition, psychology, physiology, and oppression—tend to have less Faustian jobs than men. And Faustian is where the money is" (103).

In "Women in the Locker Room!" Blount takes a magisterial view of the relationship of women and men writers to male and female sports. He asserts that Walt Whitman with his combination of masculinity and femininity would be the ideal sportswriter, and insinuates himself as an implicitly heterosexual but nevertheless surrogate Whitman. Women reporters, he says, "face the same deadlines and inside-flavor requirements that men reporters do" (39), and there is a sexual embarrassment for male sportswriters interviewing naked male athletes: "I can't claim to have felt like a woman in a men's dressing room, but I have been made to feel rather . . . chirpy, and like a second-class citizen, by players who didn't like sharing their scene with Clark Kent. An interviewee may have no towel around his waist yet still have one around his mind" (41). Women also can take pleasure in recording, as did Stephanie Salter of the *San Francisco Examiner,* some superficial, self-satisfying ironies:

Another superstar embarrassed Salter the same way he would any male reporter who pinned him down. "He was complaining about 'not being part of the offense,'" she said, "and I asked him if he was saying he was pissed off because his teammates weren't getting him the ball. He started yelling in front of everybody, 'That's exactly the kind of question—that's exactly what the press gets wrong!' And then he flounced off to the john. Later I sat down with him and got him to explain what he meant. Essentially, it was that he was pissed off because his teammates weren't getting him the ball." (42)

Not harping on the fairness of the matter, Blount says men should also be allowed in women's dressing rooms: "Presumably there would be too much ogling if a lot of male scribes were to barge into a functioning sanctum of women. But women can wear towels too, and a band of athletes has a corporate air that discourages even optical barging" (45). A great sportswriter would be interested in the physiognomy of female and male athletes and would ask the crucial sportswriting questions, as Walt Whitman had:

> *Who goes there? hankering, gross, mystical, nude;*
> *How is it I extract strength from the beef I eat?*
>
> *What is a man anyhow? What am I? what are you?* (45)

Although tangential to the male-female issue, "The Lowdown on Southern Hospitality" looks at the issue of hosts and hostesses and gives Blount a chance to say what Southerners do not admit to Northerners about one of the region's most misunderstood social customs. Although in his newer, national mode, the persona has a "certain resistance to comparisons between Southern and Northern anything," he is both a Southern host and a Northern observer of southern hospitality, and he gets back to the overriding distinction between the regions, in manners and language. The South has a tradition of hospitality born of climate and rhetoric:

In the South, people are more likely to be sitting out on the porch when folks show up. You can't pretend not to be at home, when there you are sitting on the porch. You can pretend to be dead, but then you can't fan yourself.
. . . The salesperson in Rich's Basement in Atlanta may give you just as glazed a look as the one in Filene's Basement in Boston, but the former is more likely to say, "These overalls are going to make your young one look cute as pea-turkey." Southerners derive energy from figures of speech, as plants do from photosynthesis. (28)

Southerners go out of their way to appear typical for typical Northerners who never think of themselves as typical: "If a Northern visitor makes it clear to Southerners that he thinks it would be typical of them to rustle up a big, piping hot meal of hushpuppies and blackstrap, Southerners will do that, even if they were planning to have just a little salad that night" (29). Revving up the stereotypes, Blount describes what happens after a Northerner has responded to a Southerner's protestations that he visit, and is prevailed on to stay on for a *couple* of weeks, and is allowed to leave, finally, after promising to come back soon and to bring even more relatives next time:

And the Southerners close their door. And they slump back up against it. And they look at each other wide-eyed. And they say, shaking their heads over the simplemindedness of Yankees, *"They came!"*
"And like to never left!"
"And ate us out of house and home!"
Nothing—not even the sight of people eating hushpuppies mushed up in blackstrap molasses—is sweeter than mounting irritation prolongedly held close to the bosom. (31)

How Blount can weave together the sexual, domestic, and literary strands is illustrated in another long, literary ramble written for *Play-*

boy, "I Always Plead Guilty," which relentlessly follows the thesis "Fucking up is not what it used to be" (116). In the changing times, Blount finds sources to blame for the decline of the tradition: the economy, cocaine, the legal profession, and the Reagan administration, which so skews the rhetoric that it cannot fail:

Another thing the Reagan administration is keen on is saying nasty things about Russia. Anybody in the world can think of nasty things to say about Russia. What takes imagination is thinking of things to say about Russia that aren't nasty and still make sense. Still another trick the Reagan administration has managed to pull off is to make the rich get richer and the poor get poorer. If the Reagan administration were a refrigerator, it would say that its purpose was to let ice melt. And people wonder how the president manages to stay so relaxed. (121)

The Reagan administration is enough to make a man feel depressed, which thought leads to another comment on differences between male and female sexual attitudes:

Recently, I heard a woman author tell an audience that men know nothing about friendship because they never had lunch together to tell each other how depressed they are. Well, "depressed" may be a word that women feel more comfortable with than men do. Men don't generally like to say they're depressed, not in so many words. I think you have to give men some credit for that, because there are no more boring—not to say depressing—words in English than "I am depressed." That's one of the shortcomings of *being* depressed. (121–22)

Approaching indignation at the way things are going (for men, primarily, but also for the country), Blount moves back to Reagan and the president's antithesis, the Satan of *Paradise Lost,* and recognizes what is to be gained from a clear perception and unsanctimonious expression of the hellishness in human nature, provided it does not get too Faustian:

I seem to have written myself very nearly into an identification with the Prince of Darkness. (Milton did the same thing in *Paradise Lost.*) I want to back off from that. "Sympathy for the Devil" was a callow song (especially at Altamount, when the Rolling Stones were singing it while somebody was being stabbed to death by Hell's Angels). People who actually enter hell, prison, an asylum, the courts, or delirium tremens invariably report that either heaven or workaday life is gravely preferable. I'll take their word for it. But isn't there some middle ground? Why do we have to draw back so *far* from the abyss? (129)

Without the abyss—in this book the chasm dividing and challenging the sexes—there would be no bridges for the humorist to build, no blue yodels, and no urgency about the male and female nature and modern manners. In the interludes, sketches, and essays, Blount burlesques brinkmanship by promoting *a* male point of view; he was, of course, writing when the subject was safer for humor, when it was cooling and when irony had already overtaken and modified feminist rhetoric. (Even Joanie Caucus was losing her shrillness in "Doonesbury.") Whereas Blount is bolder in raising questions than in answering them, creating characters to take positions the main persona avoids, even so, simply getting into the argument and reacting with more than sit-com superficiality was enough to tease out the partisans. Nancy A. Walker, in a study of feminist humor, found Blount's book "one of the many indications that the women's movement has done little to change women's lives, despite repeated attempts at fundamental revisions of political and social policies and attitudes."[5] To support her contention that Blount is uneasy about feminism, that he approaches feminism "as though it were equivalent to being a Democrat or a Methodist—an affiliation to be changed at will," and that he represents a "continuing resistance to the principle of gender equality," Walker cites not the main persona in the humor but Roger, the speaker in "Blue Yodel 4":

I don't understand guys who say they're feminists. That's like the time Hubert Humphrey, running for President, told a black audience that he was a soul brother.

And say you fall in love with somebody and it turns out she's not *a feminist. It happens. You've kind of painted yourself into a corner now, haven't you? What are you going to say—you've always believed in feminism but you'll give it up for her? How's she going to take that?* (31)

What Walker does not say is that at the end of an exchange between Roger the feminist and Cheryl, in which Roger embraces feminism entirely, Cheryl snaps, "Why is it so important to you?"

In a 1989 *Boston Globe* interview Blount agreed that female humorists have more license to write about male-female relationships:

Women can write angrily and be well received. Men can't. But that's the burden of being the gender in power. Actually, I wrote a book called *What Men Don't Tell Women,* and I was told by some bookstores that women resented the fact that I was being amusing about this topic. As if there were some topics that are too serious to laugh about. But my feeling is that a humorous writer should have the same kind of instinct that makes a cat go to the one person in the room who doesn't like cats—an instinct to drift toward the pressure. So if anything seems like something I should not write about, then I want to do it.[6]

The ultimate risk in writing literary humor about male-female relationships is that the treatment will be too controversial to be funny or too facetious to reflect the magnitude of the issue. Blount is creating for his readers what Freud in his essay on humor calls "the pleasure arising from an economy in the expenditure upon feeling," by describing "real and imaginary people" who do not need to (or, one might add, cannot or will not) display any humor themselves.[7] Blount's persona presumes that readers have enough irony to detach themselves from the argument, to exchange their heavier and more taxing anxieties for lighter or more "economical" laughter, and to sympathize with his efforts to make sense of a crazy time.

The kind of intellectual and emotional comic relief described by Freud did not come to all of the reviewers of *What Men Don't Tell Women.* Annie Davis of the Continuing Learning Corporation in Cambridge, Massachusetts, in an eleven-line review in *Library Journal* said that in treating topics "from Elvis to orgasm" Blount often misses the mark, that his tone "seems lacking in compassion," and that his "laughs pointed at the follies of others." Davis warned librarians: "At points, some passages border on ethnic slur, and Blount's crude vocabulary may be objectionable for some public libraries."[8]

In his review in the *New York Times,* Anatole Broyard, who had complimented Blount for *Crackers,* saw him as the victim of "occupational psychosis," no longer able to tell the difference between the ordinary and the absurd, and "like a man whose tennis court ought to have its lines refreshed." After this scolding, Broyard admitted to liking much in the book; he praised Blount for sometimes having "a sharp eye and a good ear" and found the Whitman reference "wonderful."[9]

Two weeks later, in the *New York Times Book Review,* Dan Greenburg gave the book a solid, if subjective, rave, selecting passages from the attack on the deconstruction movement in literary criticism ("What do we speak of when speak of 'literature'? Before we can begin to 'answer' that question we must ask another question: 'What do we speak of when we speak "What"?'"), the Southern hospitality essay, and the more biting parts of the blue yodels. [10] Ron Givens in *Newsweek* also selected for praise the blue yodel featuring the faithful Cooper, the Southern hospitality essay, and the Walt Whitman-as-sportswriter reference, and he came as close as any reviewer to understanding how Blount's handling of a loaded subject lifted his humor above the "quick and/or dirty approach." Givens saw that Blount was not "afraid to kick his notions around in public, with simultaneously intriguing and amusing results." [11]

The whole impression left by *What Men Don't Tell Women* is of a first-rate intelligence at play on an issue that bothers everybody. Each of the longer essays enlarges the topic under discussion, whether it be Southern hospitality, the role of women, or the size of salaries, and the interludes are like jokes (often they are jokes) that break up the one-way conversation should it threaten to become strident or tiresome. Both the essays and the interchapters are meant to be funny but not flippant. Perceptions of the issues are guided by the conversational tone of the main persona and all the blue yodelers, and that tone is the result of Blount's mastery of a prose style that conveys information and opinion, literary allusion and outrage, with such art that it rarely calls attention to itself as style. Yet it is through the conversational style that Blount makes welcome an array of readers, points up the magnitude of the issue, and encourages the willing suspension of hostilities. The speakers are too engaged in their own problems to engage the reader in anything but a humorous response; the dramatic distancing created by the characterization discharges the tension. No doubt, the primary subject unifying this collection is the role of women, which is railed at, rejected, acknowledged, accepted, and elevated by a man, though in not so tidy a progression. But the conversationalist, coming on as merely a baffled and unthreatening male, is actually the courtly lover, more confident of his ideal than of his chances of success, who is pursuing a subject that will never be consummated. The result of so many incongruities converging at once is, for both sexes, an interlude in the debate, a far-reaching, informed, and often intimate conversation, and not a little humanizing humor.

Not Exactly What I Had in Mind

Two major shifts, one cultural and the other political, give a different cast to the humor in Roy Blount's third collection: the battle between the sexes had settled into familial skirmishes and Ronald Reagan
had established himself as a power worthy of a reckoning. In addition
to being a gathering *of* humor, the anthology is also *about* humor, full
of reflections on the life of a humorist coming around to a fuller expression of himself as part of a national tradition. The persona is an established humorist, already being anthologized in "best of American
humor" collections, capable of writing about humor and of approaching a comparison of himself with Mark Twain. He is also a writer more
interested in the smaller concrete particularities of writing and family
life than in the larger abstractions and the rambling ways of the persona
in *Crackers*. Nevertheless, he has politics and the character of the
United States on his mind. Ronald Reagan, the target of glancing shots
in *What Men Don't Tell Women,* appears as a point of reference, home
base for the humor. Still not quite the complete curmudgeon, the persona is a 1960s liberal, burdened with ideals, memories, and common
sense; the collection is pitched toward the attitude expressed in its
title.

Consistent with the pattern established in the other anthologies, the
humor in *Not Exactly What I Had in Mind* (1985) shows the harvesting
of earlier work and the sowing of later. Illustrating the first is a unified
personal essay about Blount's army days, "Salute to John Wayne,"
which was started as a series of *Atlanta Journal* columns and completed,
through the use of more recent experiences and more detailed memories, in the *Atlantic* almost twenty years later. "The Roosters Don't
Like It," about sundry Georgians' reactions to daylight saving time,
also began as a *Journal* column, and the second salute in the collection,
to the late University of Alabama football coach, began as "Bear
Bryant's Stomping School," a 1977 *Esquire* column. Developing in *Not
Exactly What I Had in Mind* are sketches for public presentations—the
solution to the federal deficit ("buy stamps and throw them away"); a
barroom recital poem, "The Phantom Jukebox"; and the launderable
comments about celebrities from the *Playboy* essay "What's So Hot
about Celebs?"

Blount's opinions about Ronald Reagan were apparently already
fully formed by the time he was writing and collecting for the third
book. As simple and as complicated as Reagan himself, the opinions

do not result in the rich ruminations of *Crackers*. Obviously, Reagan represents another kind of alter ego of the persona—not a Georgian but a public performer, an actor becoming a politician as opposed to a writer becoming an actor.

Establishing an introductory tone that is as close as the persona in this collection comes to outright invective, Blount looks at the Georgians he left behind, who, with their "oral resonance," had lapsed into righteous, right-wing Babbittry, confusing love of money with love of country and seeing nothing wrong with giving money for warheads and nothing right in giving it to fatherless ghetto babies. He names those Georgians as prototypes of the incumbent: "As far as I can tell, Ronald Reagan is one of these people. Only without the oral resonance" (xiii).

Blount attacks Reagan with editorial energy and no apparent compulsion to be circuitous—a tacit concession that Reagan is too powerful and too oblivious (of almost everything) to be hurt by humor, as Carter was. To Blount, Reagan represents a "simplified celebrity" and "a kind of logo, who knows about as much about how the nation or the world functions as Betty Crocker knows about baking" (101). Though Blount writes in the introduction that he refuses to get Reagan's jokes, he is aware of the actor-president's ability to command public attention and to compete with other performers, among them humorists. "This book is not about Ronald Reagan *per se* (whatever that might mean)," says Blount. "But what I have in mind, roughly speaking, is to pull against the President's sense of humor without losing hold of mine" (xiv).

In the *New York Times* account of his 1988 stage show, Blount sounds more like Will Rogers: "It seems to me that Reagan's in the same business I am—making foolish statements. . . . If the whole Presidency had been tongue-in-cheek, it would have been brilliant. But since it was in earnest, it got my goat."[12] But in the essay on celebrity that Blount reads on an audiotape, the tone is decidedly less folksy and conciliatory: "He communicates serenity, because he isn't thoughtful enough to have any shame. He believes in his good-guy role, so why should he question himself? He was not ruffled when he called his own dog by the wrong name in front of the dog and reporters. That is what I call your definitive tinsel figure: a person who feels he can afford, psychologically, not to know his own dog" (101).

In "Why Did the President Hit Angie Dickinson?" Blount picks up an idea first dropped in the "Why I Always Plead Guilty" *Playboy* essay that is republished in *What Men Don't Tell Women*. The actor in the movie version of Hemingway's *The Killers* who had displayed his great gift, "seeming to be less out-to-lunch than he looks," had grown in the persona's mind into the even more grotesque and inaccessible president. In being able only to imagine, in the second essay, what would have happened had Reagan played the lead in *Casablanca* and Humphrey Bogart gone to the White House (Blount doesn't point up the irony in a translation), Blount encountered the same problem other humorists had with Jimmy Carter: "The fascinating thing is that there is never anything interesting to say about the Reagans. Working oneself into a lather over them is like working oneself into a lather over, say, Mickey Rooney. It's not going to do any good. Just as there are always going to be a certain number of welfare cheats, there are always going to be a certain number of people like the Reagans. It's never been my feeling that such people should be at our nation's helm, but what do I know? I'm from Georgia" (144).

Humor, Blount states in the final essay in this collection, was undergoing a resurgence, flourishing as it had during the Harding and Coolidge administrations "in times of chipper but ill-advised composure" (173). In interviews, he has cited specific examples of the flourishing, Mark Twain writing under Grant and Benchley and Dorothy Parker thriving under Coolidge.[13] Though their parallel is apt, there is little in Blount's humor that directly relates to President Reagan's policy decisions or speeches. "What You Personally Can Do about the Federal Deficit," now one of Blount's most popular stage pieces, suggests that stamps can be bought and thrown away. Refuting the objection that the post office is no longer part of the federal government, Blount likens his proposal to Reagan's ideas, which are never picked apart: "I'll tell you why, he owes everybody too much money" (5). But the essay is short (650 words) and does not analyze, scrutinize, or bemoan.

Without a negative national consensus, as he had with Jimmy Carter, Blount keeps his deepest antipathies to himself and is generally more charitable to Reagan in public than he is in print. Privately, he acknowledges the extent of his feeling toward Reagan and toward the publications that mindlessly promoted him. Successful enough to be independent, Blount stopped writing for *Parade* after the magazine "ran a suck-up story about Reagan with a picture of him pumping iron on the cover," and he lost interest in *Vanity Fair* after it ran "a suck-up story about both Reagans," with a cover photo of them dancing. "I've never been beholden to any one publication," says Blount.[14]

Openings created by Reagan were passed up; events even through 1984—Grenada, James Watt, the president's dozing, Nancy's machinations—could have been a humorist's field day. Apparently, Blount was repulsed, reluctant to get trapped in a stance, or merely defeated, or perhaps he did not want to venture into satire, which dignifies a subject and implies that the attitudes associated with it might be correctible. Reflecting on the book and Reagan, Blount said he was getting "older and more irritable" but did not want to appear bitter and doctrinaire. He called the Reagan administration "a dash of cold water" and said that not only could he "not find a toe hold" to write about Reagan but "nobody wanted me to write about him. I like to write about people I have some sympathy for, and Reagan and I weren't playing the same game. I didn't want to write dismissible, crank stuff. I felt ideological about Reagan, and ideology is seldom very funny."[15]

Although *Not Exactly What I Had in Mind* started out to "pull against" Reagan's sense of humor, Blount realized what a threat to his own Reagan's was. He was not finished by or with Reagan, as two magazine essays published shortly after the third collection and republished in the fourth indicate. In "We the People," published in the *New York Times Magazine,* the guarantees of the First Amendment are summed up in the rights of every American to say of Ronald Reagan, "I have never had any use for the son of a bitch." But Blount had recovered irony and perspective in "The Wit and Wisdom of Ronald Reagan," published in *Penthouse,* and he looked at the role of the press and the public as factors in the Reagan phenomenon—Reagan's ability to make the complex simple and vice versa, and his constant use of other people. Still, despite the parallels between Blount's favorite humorists and their Republican presidents, Ronald Reagan has not—not yet, anyway—played Calvin Coolidge to Blount's Dorothy Parker. But, unlike Carter, Reagan still looms as an annoying possibility, one Blount will come back to, as he does in *Not Exactly What I Had in Mind,* for reference.

The Reagan years raised the president as a lone target; relationships between Reagan and the mood of the times may only be inferred. Moving along in the midst of the affluent, self-indulgent decade, Blount presents himself as a settled family man, living, as E. B. White had, on a New England farm, pursuing the moderate happiness of a successful writer with his second wife and his two children, able to afford gadgets, to eat in fancy restaurants, to travel enough to write an essay on packing, and to write reviews of women's lingerie. Without admitting as much, Blount was a long way from the malaise days of the Carter administration that had invigorated his humor and lifted it to antic heights.

Blount is interested in humor, as well as in creating it, as several of the essays indicate. In particular, pieces on Erma Bombeck and Bill Murray establish a humor bracket for the times and for Blount. Bombeck he likes because, in a "time of sexual reapportionment," her humor has a "nice no-nonsense tone," but he does not like her so much that he overlooks lapses in style, when phrases, prepositional and participial, dangle for no humorous effect. Nevertheless, she "would appeal to readers of all genders even had there been no women's movement," Blount said. "But now that men's roles have all gone to hell, and every modern person who is not rich or vagrant is half housewife, we can perhaps take Bombeck's undespairing desperation to heart" (75). In dealing with comically incorrigible modern children, Blount prefers the thinking of Bombeck over that of another writer he esteems but probably would not have compared with Bombeck in *What Men Don't Tell Women,* the feminist Doris Lessing. The long profile of Murray, written in the style he had developed at *Sports Illustrated,* is more expository than personal, but Blount finds admirable in Murray a unification of the same contrary traits that make his own humor work: the combination of conventionality and flakiness, of compliance and resistance, and of detachment and involvement, as applied to art and life.

Blount's essay on Mark Twain does not presume to be a self-portrait, though he is often compared to Clemens in reviews, interviews, and blurbs. Ostensibly, the essay is a meditation following a tour of the Mark Twain house in Hartford, Connecticut. Most of the parallels are implied or played down, and Blount is too familiar with the dark side of Clemens to boast. Yet as a Southerner living in New England, Blount states an obvious reference to his own career: "Well, you may write like an angel in the South, but unless you can get those Northern publishing gears turning for you, you are not an American writer" (158). Mark Twain, like Blount, had found favor at the *Atlantic,* where, as Mark Twain expressed it, the editors "don't require a 'humorist' to paint himself striped and stand on his head every fifteen minutes."

Both were fugitives from an intolerable, oppressive, smothering South, a comparison Blount implies by quoting a Mark Twain letter written in 1876: "Ignorance, intolerance, egotism, self-assertion,

opaque perception, dense and pitiful chuckleheadedness—and an almost pathetic unconsciousness of it all. That is what I was at nineteen
and twenty; and that is what the average Southerner is at sixty today"
(159).[16] In the introduction to *Not Exactly What I Had in Mind,* Blount
uses similar cadences to defend his own flight from the South he had
known through 1968, setting Clemens's general disgust in the context
of the political mind-set that presaged Reaganism:

Years ago I left my home in Georgia, at the risk of losing touch with precious
gluons [subatomic particles] of oral resonance because in Georgia I sensed a
too-shameless concentration of people who loved to fulminate against Russia
and smut, who felt it was pusillanimous to survey the world from any other
point of view than that of the eagle on the dollar, and who seemed to feel not
only high-minded but even tingly when they looked upon the Pentagon as a
case of pure need and upon fatherless babies in the ghetto as cases of threat-
eningly unbridled self-interest. And all this in the name of Jesus. (xiii)

The hold of the South on Clemens and, by implication, Blount was
both too strong and too subtle to be broken by diatribe. "For reasons
both of the wallet and the spirit," Clemens sought popularity and
moved in the company of great writers, but, though he succeeded in
leaving the South, "his image of the people he sprang from became his
image of people in general, not to mention himself" (158–59). Blount,
whose figures of speech personify typewriters and word processors (in
this collection he makes humor of talking wrenches), also sees Clemens's love of machines as Southern, "as if they were flesh and blood and
also metaphysical. He desired an anthropomorphic machine without a
human flaw" (160).

Although Blount points out how Clemens did not trust God "any
further than he could throw Him" and how he "chaffed his beloved
wife, Livy, out of her faith, then saw her die without its consolation,"
he does not pursue the connections between the writers' similarities
and any fate they might have in common (156–57). Examination stops
before analysis and projection set in. Blount is, as the title of the essay
indicates, interested only in what makes Mark Twain "the funniest
American writer" (160).

By the time *Not Exactly What I Had in Mind* appeared, Blount's
work was also being published in general humor anthologies, and he
uses the occasion of his inclusion with sixty-three others in Mordecai
Richler's *The Best of Modern Humor* to discuss the state of humor from

a humorist's point of view. (He does not mention what is included, which is "Trash No More," from *Crackers*.)[17] Capitalizing *Humor*, he traces its history and his connections to the national tradition, beginning in high school with his reading of E. B. and Katharine S. White's *A Subtreasury of American Humor*, which was published in the year of his birth, 1941. Funny writing at the time of the Whites' anthology came out of the *New Yorker*, or appeared to, and it consisted of "parodies, sketches, personal essays, short stories, reporting, verse," which "implied a straight-faced, grateful, deftly self-conscious flouting of rigidities and . . . oh God, I've got to get out of this kind of thing" (172).

When Blount was ready to become a humorist, that style was out of vogue, though it is obvious from the list he assembled that his collections have the same generic mix, each an omnium-gatherum after the Whites' model. It took a while, however, for Blount to re-create those forms:

In high school I decided that writing Humor was my vocation. I assumed there would be a good living in it. When I got out of college in 1963, however, there was not. This was partly because I was not as good at Humor as I had been in high school and partly because of the historical moment. Humor is counterrevolutionary. So are the great majority of revolutions, within a few months, but that was not a point that seemed called for in the sixties. In the sixties we had the Theater of the Absurd and Black Humor, neither of which was funny. (173)

After J. D. Salinger and Donald Barthelme "had borne the *New Yorker* tradition of Humor off into, respectively, mysticism (or New Hampshire) and experimental fiction," humor further waned and was not revived until Philip Roth in *Portnoy's Complaint* "brought explicit sex into Humor" and Norman Mailer, referring to himself as "Mailer" and a "radical conservative" in *Armies of the Night*, added "structural drollery" (173).

Blount lists modern humorists, with a grateful acknowledgment of their contributions to the practice: Nora Ephron for showing that "matters of modern womanhood" can be resolved on the level of humor and for her "robust piece on being flatchested"; Hunter S. Thompson for taking drugs "out of the realm of stuporous religiosity" and finally "running controlled substances into the ground"; Woody Allen for bringing in Freud; Wilfred Sheed for making literary criticism funny;

Fran Leibowitz for putting "starch into Camp"; Garrison Keillor for blending "the spirits of E. B. White and St. Francis of Assisi"; and Calvin Trillin (self-styled after his column on the de la Rentas salon "Calvin of the Trillin") for finding "merriment in food, demography, and leftism" (174).

Most important, Blount ends the catalog and the kudos with his definition of the abstraction: "Whether feverish or laid-back, Humor springs from a certain desperation, which uses jujitsu on looming fear and shame, flirts almost pruriently yet coolly with madness and sentimentality, and fuses horse sense with dream logic. Asked about what it takes to write jokes, Woody Allen once replied, 'That leap. I'm scared of dead patches'" (175). And he closes his third collection by gathering together even more august humorists to complete the pantheon and to illustrate the point that "laughter is a personal matter"; he quotes Max Beerbohm's delight in the passage from Boswell in which Dr. Johnson broke up over a will written by a Mr. Chambers: "Certainly there is nothing ridiculous in the fact of a man making a will. But this is the measure of Johnson's achievement. He had created gloriously much out of nothing at all. There he sat, old and ailing and unencouraged by the company, but soaring higher and higher in absurdity, more and more rejoicing, and still soaring and rejoicing after he had gone out into the night" (175).

Not Exactly What I Had in Mind, thirty-four pieces in all, is Blount's shortest, quietest, and most subtle book. For whatever reason or complex of reasons—Ronald Reagan, Blount's increasing popularity, his personal life, his rising interest in performed humor—the third collection is the most introspective and, except for the outbursts against Reagan and the sustained reductio ad absurdum in advising the repackaging of Carl Lewis, the gentlest.

Aside from the limitations on it imposed by Reagan, Blount's literary humor is sure and quick. More secure about the voices speaking the humor, he creates some of his best fiction. "Only Hugh," about the one man in a town who refuses to be a celebrity, is a counterpart to the essay on celebrities that follows. Worthy of anthologizing again, and certain to outlast the political humor, is "Do Camp and Lit Mix? (A Letter Home)," written by "Gavin" to "Unnatural Parent," the mother who has trundled him off to Paper Mountain Writers Conference, a literary camp on Lake Sotweed, where an Avis shuttle-bus driver is writing roundels; where Gavin's adviser, "Edward Noone, the author of *Hurled,*" never head of Scott ("Scott Spencer?") and does know

Sir Walter from Edmund; and where "Reid Whiteblood, the tenured South Carolinian ironist . . . chairs our daily neo-ambiguity sessions." Among such people who shrink "at the merest whiff of esemplastic sweep," Gavin is forced to listen to "a married couple who have been driving around the nation eating chocolate chip cookies *du pays*, taking copious notes, and working up a guidebook they plan to turn into a musical about a couple falling in love while searching America for the perfect cookie." The book's working title is "Looky!" (153). Beset by mosquitoes and minimalists, Gavin hopes his mother is satisfied.

Catching the changes in tone in the new collection, Colin McEnroe in the *Hartford Courant* noted that Blount was "more consistently funny and eloquent than ever, although perhaps not quite as incandescent as he was, on a more sporadic basis, a few years back," but he also saw that Blount was including "more stinging sociopolitical commentary per square joke than ever before."[18] In the *New York Times Book Review*, Patrick F. McManus, himself a humorist, saw how Blount had raised the specter of Reagan but, fortunately for the humor's sake, had abandoned it. Slipping in his own pun, McManus defined the "Chinese water torture" effect of Blount's style, "the unceasing drip-drip-drip of bizarre images, intricate word play, droll asides, crazy ideas" that "disorients the reader until Mr. Blount finally has him at his mercy."[19]

Now, Where Were We?

Roy Blount's first three collections anticipate public appearances but are principally the work of a writing man. The fourth, which is equally literary, is nevertheless dominated by the role of the performer, who comes on as a stage character with a consistent tone, a store of anecdotes, and a ready-to-entertain manner. By the time *Now, Where Were We?* was published in 1988, Blount had already become a twentieth-century version of the literary comedian; he had served his term as a regular on Garrison Keillor's "A Prairie Home Companion," had had a successful run off-Broadway in "Roy Blount's Happy Hour and a Half," and was appearing on a variety of television programs. In the fourth collection, the literary comedian appears to be discovering and applying the materials of the literary humorist. After a lifetime of striving to be a complete humorist, in print and in person, Blount had obviously arrived. He had attracted both readers and listeners, and the widely reviewed, generally praised books and the public presentations on stage, radio, and television had, together, created a momentum for his career. Blount had also perfected the persona and the oral-but-literary routine so that the writer and the performer were fixed in a symbiotic relationship, the one informing the subject matter and influencing the style of the other.

In more than dust-jacket blurbs, Blount was being called one of the country's great humorists. Sufficient proof of his success was a full-page review of *Now, Where Were We?*, including excerpt and interview boxes, in the *New York Times Book Review*. Deborah Mason, a former *Vogue* editor, described Blount as "a self-styled rube with an agile intellect and a scatty imagination" and said his principal achievement in the collection was "the exquisite honing of his wiliest persona: professional cracker." A succession of characterizations shows how the steady flow of essays, books, and appearances had established that persona— "plain-spoken bumpkinhood," "foxy yokelism," "*faux* hayseed persona," "genial Mason-Dixon line straddler and perennial fence mender," "yokel stranger in a strange land," and "chronic outsider." Making a convincing comparison between Blount of *Now, Where Were We?* and Mark Twain of *The Innocents Abroad*, Mason called the pieces "brilliantly loopy, reassuringly subversive, and they put Mr. Blount in serious contention for the title of America's most cherished humorist."[20]

The book is similar in structure and context to *One Fell Soup*; a gathering of recent newspaper and magazine pieces, it is presented with great élan and, with the exception of the two principal references to Reagan, some apparent joy that the 1980s are nearing an end. Blount told the *New York Times Book Review* interviewer that the title of the book referred to the "end of the Reagan illusion," elaborating, "We're emerging from the past eight years as if we're coming out of a movie theater in the afternoon and blinking in the sunlight and feeling sort of ashamed of where we've just been. Reaganism was a kind of profligate narrow-mindedness; my hope is that now we'll pick up the pieces and go back to being traditional liberals and traditional conservatives."[21]

In the role of editorial commentator, Blount seems more directly engaged with immediate events around him; he is less introspective, less brooding, but older, wiser, and, in ways that Reagan was not, more conservative. The publications from which the pieces were collected indicate a firm hold on a national readership and a new address to Southern readers. Of the forty-seven pieces, ten appeared first in the *Atlantic,* six in *Condé Nast's Traveler,* four in *Gentleman's Quarterly,* four in the *San Francisco Examiner,* three in *TV Guide,* three in *Esquire,* and two in *Southern, the New York Times Magazine, and the New York Times*

Book Review; single essays appeared in the *Atlanta Journal-Constitution*, *Atlanta Weekly*, *Penthouse*, *USA Today*, *Food and Wine*, *New York*, *Sports Illustrated*, *Antaeus*, *Spy*, and *Think*, an IBM publication; and one, on "boredom," was written for but never published by *Playboy*.

From Blount's omnibus of conversational pieces, light verse, travel columns, editorials, and reviews emerges a set of central concerns: about literary values, about flushing out phonies, about health and aging, about the movement of the country, and, in particular, about the direction of his generation. Although Blount is also concerned about politics, Reagan's retirement gave him a respite; he kept making the occasional swipe at Reagan, but his attention turned to general matters. More the cultural conservative (or gentle radical) than the political liberal, Blount often explores connections and compromises— between past and present, youth and middle age, home and travel, and technology and humanity. The tendency to make peace out of conflict is not new to his humor, but in the fourth collection he seems more certain of his authority as interlocutor and arbiter. Larger, national abstractions occupy his mind, a development represented by the evolution of cover art for the collections. Portraits of the good old boy in the equipment-company cap (*One Fell Soup*) give way to images of the herringbone-coated yuppie (*Not Exactly What I Had in Mind*) that yield to a fourth-collection dust jacket showing Blount in a sports coat and William Hurt eyeglasses, eavesdropping and taking notes, diminished before a painting of the Founding Fathers signing the Constitution. The book's slogan suggests, in all capital letters, Blount's angle on conservatism: "GETTING BACK TO BASIC TRUTHS THAT WE HAVE LOST SIGHT OF THROUGH NO FAULT OF MY OWN."

The persona in Blount's travel pieces is clearly out to have fun and to make fun—of vanities and indulgences—by participating in rather than condemning them. A tone setter for the anthology is "I Find Myself at a Spa?," a thirty-five-hundred-word essay written for *Condé Nast's Traveler*. Prompting the heightening of health consciousness is the fear of death, made explicit by denial: "True, my grandfather died of a heart attack at seventy while working in the yard, and my father of a heart attack at sixty after working in the yard, but I figured I could evade that trap by staying out of the yard" (24). Holding that "it is morally wrong to eat with an ulterior motive," Blount trims down and perks up after following the diet-and-exercise regimen but does not lose his irony:

You ought to look at me! It's incredible! I look eight years younger! You ought to listen to me talk about it! I would bore your ass off! Speaking of which, I have—for me—hardly any ass left. I who can't stand people who have hardly any ass!

I would rather have Fatty Arbuckle's body than Sly Stallone's! I would rather have Fatty Arbuckle's *career*! I have never known anybody whose body was perfect-looking who was worth a shit. (21)

One basic truth Blount returns to is the ambiguity of the South. The tone in *Crackers* and in several pieces in the other three collections, most notably in the Mark Twain essay in *Not Exactly What I Had in Mind,* barely conceals an ethnic self-loathing, made tolerable by some relief at having escaped a literary but socially and intellectually blighted land. In the fourth collection, the tone is more ameliorative, and Blount is more comfortable with his Southernness and generally less critical of the section. (The poem, "A Verse to the New South," does not quite live up to the pun in its title.) This shift in attitude is probably related to Blount's emergence as a literary comedian, specifically his appearances on "A Prairie Home Companion." Like the Southerners in the hospitality essay in *What Men Don't Tell Women,* he could not come out on the national front porch, speak with his accent, and pretend not to be a Southerner.

Blount's relationship to the South as a region, and as home, is, like Garrison Keillor's relationship to Minnesota, filtered, affectionate, and occasionally wistful. The introductory essay in *Now, Where Were We?* appeared first in an election supplement distributed by the *Atlanta Constitution-Journal* at the Democratic Party National Convention in August 1988. The title reflects the folksy tone of Keillor's radio monologues: "Why It Looks Like I Will Be the Next President of the United States, I Reckon."

Confident that he will not be taken as merely a Southerner, Blount can identify himself as one, and as a Southern writer, who will settle for Eisenhower's salary as president and capitalize on the twisted language of the Reagan administration:

And I pledge this to you:

When I am elected I will honor the office by staying in it. Out of America's way. Ronald Reagan has already demonstrated that the president who seems to get the most things done is the president who lets things go.

He was good at that because he was an actor. I'll be good at it because I'm a writer. Four years at $75,000 per is a heck of a book advance. I'll bet three-fourths of Southern literature was produced for less than $300,000, all together. I'm going to *write* my presidency. And you won't have to worry about how I'm doing till the book comes out, in the fall of 1992. (10)

In "My Place among the Founding Fathers," from *Think,* Blount imagines himself as "the only Deep Southern member" of the Massachusetts delegation to the Constitutional Convention and therefore able to "depend on neither slavery nor Calvinism for my life-style" (42). He mentions a real delegate, who might be a real, if distant-in-time relative, William Blount of North Carolina, who became the first governor of Tennessee and a U.S. senator and then conspired with the British to attack the Spaniards at Pensacola and New Orleans: "Word got out. Britgate. Blount was impeached and expelled from the Senate" (45). He closes with the frightening thought that he might *be* William Blount and thus returns the persona to the role of American alien.

"I Don't Eat Dirt Personally," another essay bridging North and South, supplies a central anecdote for Blount's stage show. A *New York Times* story with the headline "SOUTHERN PRACTICE OF EATING DIRT SHOWS SIGNS OF WANING" sets the persona off on an encounter with the Northern temperament. Realizing that denying that he ever ate dirt will make Northerners accuse him of being both "Southern *and* inauthentic," the Southerner not only professes to eating dirt but compares eating "blackened red dirt" with the Northerners' consumption of sushi, which, as he tells it in a sidebar anecdote, is simply a Japanese commercial ploy to dupe Yankees. In a manner worthy of the Old Southwest humor picaro-conmen at their best, the persona hits on an even better plan than that of the Japanese:

But of course sushi was dead now, I told this Northerner, and people were Cajuned out, and even New Zealand cuisine was about to go the way of Australian, and now this hot New Guinea place, Yam Yam, was so overpraised, I figured the time was ripe for investing in dirt restaurants.

None of the Northerners I used this tack on had realized that it was time to be Cajuned out, even. The best way to get a Northerner to believe something is to talk to him as if you assume that he knows it already and that most people don't. I raised $3,800 in one evening. I figure when these investors came to me wondering what had happened to their money, I could admit that dirt-dining wasn't quite happening yet after all—that when they had invested in it, it had been ahead of its time. Which would have consoled them more than you might think. (49)

Never one to defend the South, except against certain straw Yankees raised by the humor, Blount in "Reb Banner Unloaded" makes it clear that he is no apologist for the Lost Cause. This strongly opinionated essay, directed at regional sympathizers, was written for *Southern* magazine, which was bought by the *Southern Living* conglomerate and renamed *SOUTHPOINT*; it later folded. The persona does not harangue the typical pushy Northern woman who wants to know why the South needs a flag, though he could have responded, "That's because the North isn't a place. . . . It's just a direction out of the South." The reasons for his reticence run deep: "I have a strong enough tendency to get recalcitrant when Northerners say things about the South, even when I agree with them. I don't need to be wasting powder and shot over the damn Confederate flag" (161). At the heart of the essay is the serious question of the flag's divisiveness, which Blount defines directly: "Every flag is loaded, but this one, whether its champions realize it or not (and many of them do), is loaded with antiintegrationism. Whatever your politics are, I don't see how you can disagree that a flag ought to bring the people under it together. A confederacy is a union. A regional union that dispels citizens of the region without whom there would have been no cotton or rock 'n' roll—or any Atlanta, as we know it—is pretty sorry" (162). The humorous solution is a new flag, and Blount offers three suggestions. The first flag might be adorned with a slogan similar to the name of Keillor's Lake Wobegone grocery: "Just a Pretty Good Part of the Country"; the second might be a baked sweet potato, opened, with butter oozing into it, over the words "Don't Tread on Me"; and the third might feature hands, brown and white, waving, with a slogan "that is proud but not swaggering, clever but not letting on, truly polite but not truly humble, outgoing but sufficiently selfish"—"Just Fine, and You?" (163).

Writing from California, where he was guest columnist for two weeks for the *San Francisco Examiner,* Blount teased the topic of "sodomy in a family newspaper" through three columns, but in the fourth he did discuss the topic and found yet another Southern connection, with Georgia, the state whose sodomy law the U.S. Supreme Court refused to overturn. Humoring a readership that included a large and politically powerful homosexual community, Blount establishes his own attitude before indicating how carefully he has considered the morally complex issue: "I have a confession to make here. Watching two men cuddle, even, gives me the willies. But I figure that's my problem. I tried not to let it interfere with my appreciation of the movie *My Beautiful Laundrette,* which I though was art; willies notwithstanding, it made my heart jump. The Supreme Court decision made it sink" (88). Pointing out that sodomy may be both homo- and heterosexual in the laws of some states, Blount writes that in Georgia "sodomy raises its head whenever anyone's genital factor touches anyone else's anal or oral," and he offers an insightful analysis of the problem of dealing with it, socially and legally:

What we have here is confusion of two things: the specter of sodomy and the practice of it. The specter is like the Drug Menace or Muammar al-Qaddafi, in providing an outlet for Americans' need to revile. (Specters corrupt.) The practice of sodomy is like public opinion, in that no given American is likely to be enthusiastic about the whole spectrum—but to say one band of the spectrum makes you or me blanch (small b) is not to say that there should be a law against its making my or your day. When the law proscribes certain bans, it's discriminatory (which, currently, is okay with the Supreme Court). When it outlaws the whole spectrum, whom is it trying to kid? (89)

Blount's opinions on literary matters are also well supported and not glossed over by humor. In "The Wind Rewound," he hits deconstructionism again, in a critique of *Gone with the Wind*'s sequel. The critic writes, "It is either 1890 or 1980, and a frowsy, dispirited Scarlett is cranking out a metafictional memoir of her declining years—or is she?" The characters keep talking back to Scarlett, "but does she put these words into their mouths or do they speak them of own accord so as to cast their narrator in a more interesting light?" The sequel is becoming "a mess and a disgrace, and nobody is making any bones about *that* except old General Reader, a recurrent voice reduced to a litany of 'Sho nuff, I reckon. I don't rightly know.'" To make matters more complicated, Rhett, a character-within-a-character who is asked if people ever tell him he looks like Clark Gable, is wearing a T-shirt that says, "*Today* is another day," and Prissy is saying, "Lawsy, Miss Scahlit, I don't know nothin' 'bout bein' no stereotype, I am a human being with my own inner feelings and aspirations" (155–56).

In a review for *USA Today,* Blount drops the deconstructionist mask to become the conventional critic in dismembering Rita Mae Brown and her novel *High Hearts.* Using "my daddy down in Georgia" as a foil, ostensibly disregarding his advice never to "read a Civil War novel longer than *The Red Badge of Courage,*" Blount wonders what "daddy" would have thought about a bisexual, radical feminist with an Amish father and Southern mother who studied English and classics at New York University, earned a Ph.D. from the Institute for Policy Studies, and served on the literature panel of the National Endowment for the Arts. After Blount takes up Brown's story of a woman who cuts her hair, enlists in the Confederate cavalry to be near her husband, and turns out to be the better soldier, there is little wondering about his opinion. He reads through "bad black English, caked blood, good Virginia soil, and bad white English; pausing only to note that at three different points in the first eighty-one pages someone was described as not having the sense God gave a goose." He slogs through dangling modifiers ("Shod a week ago, these shoes fit him perfectly") and "dialogue that would chip a beaver's teeth." Blount singles out one character's observation—"Man can live without pleasure, but doan know if he can live without the future"—and adds his comment: "Not for long, anyway." He pleads earnestly to the readers of *USA Today*: "You are young. I have lived through 464 pages of the past and the past perfect, indiscriminately mixed. *Listen to me.* I don't care who wrote it, don't read a Civil War novel longer than *The Red Badge of Courage*" (159).

Two essays written for the *New York Times Book Review* show Blount's skill as a literary humorist at its height. In "Exercise Books Aren't Aerobic," he imagines how such books would read if they were written by Ralph Waldo Emerson, Emily Dickinson, Edgar Allan Poe, T. S. Eliot, Flannery O'Connor, Robert Lowell, and E. E. Cummings. O'Connor, for instance, would have written, "The no-armed man was doing his lift-ups the first time he saw Elbalene Verge come looming up the baked clay road. She was jogging, larger and larger, and larger yet, till she stopped and there she stood. 'Mercy in this world,' she said when she got her breath. 'If you ain't purely something. You ever had a faith kinesiologist pop your neck?'" (138). In "Summer Time and the Reading Is Heavy," Blount posits the thesis that summer is the time for heavy reading "that works up a sweat," and he advises the reading of Proust, Melville (*Pierre; or, The Ambiguities*), the deconstructionists, the *Cantos* of Ezra Pound, and other real and weighty books. Then he invents some new, heavy reading, including *Life's Adjustable of Chaos,* by Vliet Von Vargueles, and shows how to apply incremental repetition to humor:

> You thought *Finnegan's Wake* drove you crazy? Did you keep thinking, while reading *Finnegan's Wake,* "If I could just come upon one straight phrase, even, that just sort of sounds like a normal person communicating"? Well, this new book is even more so, and longer. So rife is this new book with quintuple semi-entendres that if you could get cable television where you are, you would throw this book away. If the bluefish were biting where you are, you would throw this book away. If any halfway decent-looking sand dollars ever washed up where you are, you would throw this book away. And yet, you find yourself not throwing this book away. Because it is literally too heavy (239)

(A "rather pleading letter" inserted in the review copy by the author's wife explains that the book title is a pun on "Life is just a bowl of cherries.")

At the end of *Now, Where Were We?,* Roy Blount had cleared the problem of dealing with Reagan and had confirmed that humor, not satire, was his métier. Readers of the fourth collection encounter a persona of high intelligence and broad experience who reflects the social, political, and intellectual life of a generation and a class. Baby boomers who have the worries and the wit to be on Blount's wavelength meet a sensibility that has participated completely in their times, a writer and thinker who is capable of being funny without trivializing experience or evading serious principles. Readers thus engaged by the persona's ability to create humor by relating the high and the low, the exotic and the domestic, and the common and the literary had already become the core of an audience predisposed to be entertained when the persona appeared in public as the literary comedian.

Chapter Seven

The Literary Comedian: "Roy Blount's Happy Hour and a Half"

I've always felt comfortable in front of a crowd.
—Roy Blount, Jr.

Guides cannot explain the subtleties of the American joke.
—Mark Twain, *The Innocents Abroad*

Writing humor was not enough for the great nineteenth-century humorists, and it has not been enough for Roy Blount, Jr., their twentieth-century counterpart. The country's first literary comedians went on the platform to make money, and a host of them succeeded, most notably Mark Twain, who recouped a fortune on the national circuit. Though it is reasonable to assume that literary comedians possess the same personal and pecuniary motives as other actors, some special factors encouraged the earlier writer-humorists to take to the stage, or the performers to publish. For one, a pen name and a stage name indicated that the writer-actor had created a dramatis persona, a mask to stand for him, as Josh Billings did for Henry Wheeler Shaw, Petroleum V. Nasby for David Ross Locke, and Artemus Ward for Charles Farrar Browne. In addition, the literary comedians discovered the symbiotic relationship that can exist between written and spoken humor: what works on the page may be reshaped for rendering and, likewise, routines that succeed on the stage may be extended for print and sold again. For the humorist who was primarily a comedian, the printed word framed the performance, serving art and mammon, as a rehearsal and a repository and as advertisement and follow-up. The nineteenth-century literary comedians demonstrated that once a persona or mask becomes popular, less effort is needed to sustain it. (The other side of this dramatic inertia, as Johnson Jones Hooper discovered before the Civil War and Mark Twain after, is that once that persona is fixed in

the public mind, it can become an iron mask.)[1] For the literary comedians, the prose and performed humor contributed to an artistic and
commercial momentum—for the rising humorist, a happy union between art and a good living.

The apotheosis of this people's humorist, and the one whose career
Roy Blount's most closely resembles, is Mark Twain, who was so favored by the nation that the cigar named for him was sold in a box
bearing the slogan "Known by Everyone, Loved by All." A quarter-
century after Clemens's death, Will Rogers, of lesser stature but still
an American of the West who succeeded in the East, occupied his
place. After radio and the movies had replaced vaudeville and the en-
tertainment-lecture tour, the role of literary comedian divided: for example, nationally known literary humorists of the Algonquin–*New
Yorker* set were, with the exception of Benchley, writers only, and comedians were primarily radio and movie actors, with no need to publish, who could hire writers if they wanted fresh material. The advent
of television has enforced that division; writers for such comedians as
Johnny Carson are names in the credits.

Given a century of changes in American literature and entertain-
ment, it is a surprise that a writer of Roy Blount's skill and stature
would approach the old role of literary comedian and play it as Browne,
Locke, and Shaw had. Reviewers have seen Blount's humor as analo-
gous to that of Mark Twain and Will Rogers without knowing how
deep the analogy runs. Because Blount has not achieved the popularity
of the now largely unknown nineteenth-century humorists—Lincoln
read his cabinet a passage from Artemus Ward before reading them the
final draft of the Emancipation Proclamation—a comparison of
Blount's career with earlier literary comedians' might seem, at the moment, farfetched.[2] Though Blount is skilled at writing and performing
humor, he is not yet a master of the dominant medium of his time,
television, as Clemens was of print and Rogers of radio and movies,
and he has held back from making the kind of satiric comments that
endear Mark Twain to us now but were not considered a significant
part of his humor during his own lifetime. Although like Browne,
Locke, and Clemens, Blount has cultivated a following by moving
from journalism to written humor and, finally, to literary comedy, he
has also not become a household name. Still, Blount is like those icon-
oclastic, wry "phunny phellows"; though hardly the benign and beloved pundit, he is redefining the role of the single performer, whose
material and perspective are his own.

In Blount's case, it seems logical that he should progress to the role of literary comedian. The nature of his writing, dominated as it is by a persona that usually directly addresses a reader, is dramatic and conversational, and it seems to urge on performance as a way of completing the social act of humor. The persona in Blount's humorous sketches seeks public approval, the feel of the crowd, and the confirmation of laughter. In pieces that often read like dramatic monologues, the prose creates an independent but sympathetic reader-listener, one who is defined, addressed, and humored. That reader is essentially on a level with the writer, and the comedian, for his part, also levels with the listener. Both are, in fact, educated musers in a midlife morass of aging, parenting (often single), trying to maintain a marriage or a "relationship," and searching for a way to cope with (and language to suitably describe) life in America in the late twentieth century. Rather than being despondent, however, the writer (and, by extension, the reader or the listener) is engaged with life and literature; keen on what is happening in politics, sports, and technology; and able to pick up the passing allusion to "Dover Beach."

Since Blount's prose does not conform to conventional literary genres—not only does it not conform; it deliberately distorts the essay, the short story, and the poem, and creates humor thereby—performance also represents a way of making humor into a completed literary and dramatic act. Performance has a demonstrable structure, a beginning, middle, and end; the comedian represents the audience in a conflict with the world, and what he makes of that conflict leads toward a resolution. By the end of the presentation, humor may be seen in the context of comedy, a form that culminates in the relief of anxiety and the recovery of a certain peace of mind. Troubles with travel, children, and sundry changes are reduced by laughter and by language. In his stage show, Blount parodies dramatic structure by exposing a list of literary terms on an easel by his lectern (*catastrophe, deus ex machina, dramatic irony*), and he crosses them off as he proceeds through the show, though not all the devices are demonstrated on stage. In the public performance, Blount's contrapuntal written humor—its two primary elements being the persona and all the incongruities he ponders—attracts a third component, the crowd, which tests the humor and decides what is funny.[3]

Whatever the reasons for its existence, Blount's career as a literary comedian has a long foreground. With the encouragement of his mother and the example of his father, he was pointed toward the role of performer and public man. As he notes in the "Person and Persona" chapter of this book, the recitations he performed taught him how laughter could be created from sorrow—and he obviously enjoyed the power to make people laugh. Though the persona in his prose humor may seem diffident and the stage humorist reluctant to entertain, Blount was apparently born with the instinct to perform.[4] He was president of his senior class and a leader in church youth groups; at Vanderbilt he participated in public debates on the integration issue and rose to editor of the student newspaper.[5] His father's position as a leader in the Atlanta metropolitan area provided an additional motivation for Blount, not simply toward making a name for himself but also toward civic action. In his role as humorist, Blount has never forsaken the ethical mission of the editorial writer called to speak out on matters of public welfare. Even though what he makes of issues might be humor, which issues he selects indicates an eye for the significant and the serious, and the solutions he suggests—for instance, a Southern flag saying "Just Fine, and You?" to replace the divisive Confederate battle flag—illustrate long thinking about important, complicated matters.

Blount's stage career has developed from book promotion tours, which have involved speaking to booksellers and readers and submitting to countless radio, television, and newspaper interviews. For the *Crackers* promotion in 1980, he appeared on "The Dick Cavett Show." By 1990, he had appeared about thirteen times, by his count, on Johnny Carson's "The Tonight Show." Additional appearances include "Late Night with David Letterman" (first on 16 February 1983), Ted Koppel's "Nightline," "Austin City Limits," "The CBS Morning Program" (now defunct), "The CBS Morning News," the televised version of "A Prairie Home Companion," and several other programs. The appearances sell books and promote Blount's public performances, and they also provide a chance for testing the humor before the host, the studio audience, and the nation. "They are tricky to do," Blount says. "But sometimes you have the sense that you are talking to the country."[6]

Though he has never had a single big break, appearances on Garrison Keillor's National Public Radio program, "A Prairie Home Companion," beginning in 1981 and running through the show's closing in 1987, fixed Blount's reputation with millions of listeners and readers. The association began after Keillor wrote Blount a letter complimenting him for some pieces in the *New Yorker*. The two exchanged visits—

Keillor to Blount's home in Mill River, Massachusetts, and Blount to Keillor's in Minneapolis–St. Paul—and Blount appeared on the show for the first time on 30 May 1981. Over the six years, he appeared with, among others, Ernest Tubb, Sidney Pollock, Kim Stanley, Chet Atkins, Johnny Gimble, Robin and Linda Williams, and Jean Redpath and had played several characters—among them Thoreau, the Prodigal Son, one of the several foolish virgins, and a pig.[7] On 24 January 1987, when Blount was snowed in following a flight from Europe, he spoke to the radio audience by phone from New York.[8] When Keillor closed the show on 13 June 1987, to seek a new life in Denmark (from which he returned to begin a new program in 1989), Blount offered a valedictory poem, one stanza of which reads:

> Toothache's deep-rooted but bliss is a rover—
> A time comes to bid it so long.
> It's better for something to be good and over
> Than awful and still going strong.

Blount came into his own as a solitary stage performer with "Roy Blount's Happy Hour and a Half," which ran at the American Place Theatre, off-Broadway, for thirteen performances, from 22 January to 7 February 1988, as the twenty-sixth in the theater's American Humorists' Series.[9] The show resulted from a two-week, 1986 run of "Laugh at Lunch," a brown-bag performance that Blount suggested to director Wynn Handman. Edith Oliver in the *New Yorker* called it "the most humorous and engaging 50 minutes in town" (a comment Blount included in the third-person autobiographical sketch he wrote for the *Playbill* for his 1988 show) and said that Blount's "anecdotes, set in his native Georgia or in Massachusetts, are always pointed and funny, and his delivery is dead on target."[10] The "Happy Hour and a Half" performance, also directed by Handman, was done at night, before an audience of about fifty.

Praise from four New York reviewers indicate how successfully Blount drew on the "capital accrued in writing."[11] He was identified as simple but intelligent, Southern but national. In the first *New York Times* review, Leslie Bennetts focused on Blount's successful handling of his "misadventures." For the performance she attended, he told the story of the piranha attack in the Amazon and of trying to outspend Elizabeth Taylor's $2,500 bill for a day's room service at the Plaza Athenee. (The story, "I Just Want What Liz Always Has," is, like many of those in the stage show, from *Now, Where Were We?*) Bennetts was familiar enough with Blount's writing to see the performer as a writer. "Mr. Blount, who was born in Decatur, Ga., has long exhibited a keen, multi-faceted intelligence," she wrote, adding that "his books attest to the breadth of his interests."[12] The next day, Mel Gussow, in another *Times* review, liked everything from the title to Blount's style of interweaving anecdotes; he concluded, "For someone profitably employed in 'the humor line,' he is most engaging company."[13] Leo Seligsohn in *Newsday* found Blount "a talented, entertaining, low-keyed, grass-roots humorist" and wrote: "An ordinary-looking fellow wearing glasses, jacket, slacks and an open shirt, he's a gentle reminder of the difference between humorists, of which America has few, and comedians, who seem to be everywhere. Unlike the latter, who travel the fast lanes of show biz firing punch lines, Blount engages in slow-talking story telling. Simple and unadorned, the show has the sound and look of a college lecture."[14] The *Daily News* reviewer, David Hinckley, described Blount's style as the "slow, precise manner of a man who's formulating the thought as he speaks it," with a format drawn from "observations, as he segues from family stories to lamentations about the plight of the singing impaired."[15]

Blount considers the "Happy Hour and a Half" presentation the high point of his "standing-there-talking-in-front-of-you career" and also suggests how public performance influences the changes evident in his latest collection:

I am a talking writer, like a singing cowboy, sort of, only a singing cowboy is actually a singer on horseback—I am a writer on stage or camera or microphone. Or a talker, rather: it's an extension of sitting around drinking and telling stories amongst sportswriters. Performing is more fun than writing, but I can never aspire to the kind of control as a performer that I aspire to as a writer. I've always thought of writing as a form of speech, of address, and performing may have loosened and fluidized my writing some, I don't know; but I still think of writing as talking better than you can talk orally. I can't do justice orally to what I can hear or to what I can get down in letters.[16]

However successful Blount may have been with his off-Broadway show and subsequent lecture-circuit appearances that represent variations and updates of that presentation, public performance imposes limitations not covered in his self-analysis. In a world saturated with televised humor, from reruns of "Laugh-in" and "Second City Television" to newer improvisational and stand-up broadcasts, and with storefront comedy clubs flourishing in bigger cities, individuals succeed by creating special identities. For example, Gilda Radner, a comedian Blount profiled in a cover story for *Rolling Stone* in 1978, found a dominating identity in the character of Roseanne Roseannadanna, the observer of minutiae on "Saturday Night Live," and it was for this impersonation that she was remembered and praised following her death eleven years later.[17] It is ironic that Blount, when he came to the stage, would draw his dramatic strength from his Southernness. Throughout much of his writing, especially through *Not Exactly What I Had in Mind,* he has anguished, with varying degrees of seriousness, over the South and his relationship to it and, in his writings, has found ways to sidestep the identification when he wants to. On the stage, however, the sound of his voice is tantamount to auto-casting, an instant characterization to be dealt with and explained. In presenting himself as a Southern type, Blount found a way to get around the stereotypes by presenting a stage character that is both Southern and different—not a buffoon or a rube to be laughed at but a sensibility to be recognized and laughed with.

Audiences with expectations drawn from several generations of comedians encounter in Blount not the neurotic, flibbertigibbet brilliance of Woody Allen or the counterculture cynicism of George Carlin but instead a Southerner—yet one who is not like Brother Dave Gardner, the preacher-turned-bad, or Jerry Clower, the feed-and-seed-store raconteur. In the role of reasonably laid-back but worried person, Blount undercuts the role of stage Southerner; he defends the South only against offensive Northerners, to whom he is respectful but not submissive. Blount's regionalism provides a sadness, a self-loathing, and a wellspring of language (the equivalent of Allen's Jewishness and Richard Pryor's blues); it is the burden of Southern history borne north, where Americans are also heavy laden but do not always know it. Thus Blount tells them how Northern behavior on subways and streets looks to a Southerner who has no right to judge anybody else's manners and how everyday Northern speech, so spare of metaphors, sounds to one with a birthright of figurative language. He also can show how to put on Yankees who think that all Southerners are geophagists by telling a version of "I Don't Eat Dirt Personally," from *Now, Where Were We?*

Blount's accent is not spectacularly Southern (to a Southerner); it is neither of the old, disappearing, aristocratic strain that Mark Twain described in *Life on the Mississippi* (Clemens wrote, "The educated Southerner has no use for an 'r,' except at the beginning of a word," and he probably said, for effect, *wuh-id*) nor of the harder and twangier Appalachian strain. The first accent, bastardized and exaggerated, which once dominated Southern comic caricatures from Senator Phogbound to Foghorn Leghorn—"Ah say, son"—gave way to the second, personified in the accents of Andy Griffith and Jim Nabors. Blount's is a middle-class, modern, suburban Georgia accent, not as affected and idiosyncratic as James Dickey's or as soft and shrill as Jimmy Carter's but easy to identify as generally Southern by Northern audiences. Blount's voice, both deep and nasal, is described by his old Vanderbilt buddy and admirer, former Tennessee governor Lamar Alexander, as a "rumble."[18] Though it might be influenced by Bear Bryant and the other football coaches and country characters Blount has written about, the stage voice is not gruff, assertive, or stylized. If his lack of dramatic presence moves the audience to think he is not ready for the New York stage, he says, by way of opening, "Don't think I don't know what you mean."

In person, Blount is the Southern journalist telling stories to the enlightened equals inferred in the prose humor. (Despite the "happy hour" in the title, the set is a lecture hall.) Dressed like an aging preppy in a blazer and wire-rimmed glasses, he is pleasant company, and then, it turns out, he is funny—but *thoughtfully* funny, an intelligent but not intimidating, agenda-less fellow, one who is not trying too hard to impress and who has an amused but detached view of life, including his own. He doesn't smile much and does not laugh at his own stories. What he has to say is interesting, first of all, and somehow central, and, while he is doing all the talking, the sense is created that he is also listening. (Near the middle of "Happy Hour and a Half," Blount opens the floor for questions, explaining that if such a device has been used in *Othello*, "a tragedy might have been averted," which, he explains further, is why he is using the device.)

The butt of the humor is often the writer, who sometimes bumbles as Benchley did, but he is no more the Little Man than any average person, and the situations in which he finds himself are as much the world's fault as his own. The humor on the stage, like that in the writing, is cumulative. Audiotapes of Blount's performances indicate a scattered but constant level of laughter, never an explosion from one great joke.

Reviewers and the audience liked especially the humor Blount made from the remarks by CBS sports commentator Jimmy the Greek Snyder, who said that black athletes are superior to whites because selective breeding of top physical specimens of slaves had produced longer thighs.[19] Blount's handling of the episode on stage is too casual to reveal either his long association with the topic of racism or the careful way in which he establishes a basis other than self-righteous, Yankee Puritanism for his gentle humor. Snyder was fired by CBS just as Blount's show opened, providing the literary comedian with a topical subject he had already treated (though it is doubtful anyone in the audience knew how much Blount in 1973 sounded like Snyder). Blount realized, as Jimmy the Greek apparently did not, that *racial* and *racist* are virtually synonymous in the media mind. In *About Three Bricks Shy of a Load,* Blount said, in the passage quoted in chapter four of this study, "Black athletes look and move better than white ones on the average." Moreover, he did not see "anything invidious" in the notion that blacks have longer Achilles tendons. He turned the situation into humor by quoting a friend who pointed out that the comparison (in 1973) meant that Ethel Waters could jump higher than Kate Smith.

In his stage humor, Blount sets up the remarks on Jimmy the Greek by identifying himself as a "white person from the South" who was not "implicated in slavery," and he softens the blow to come, universalizing prejudice by relating it to gender. The transcript of an audiotape of the 6 February 1988 show indicates where the audience laughed as Blount turned the humor away from the obvious, superficial cheap shot: "Everybody thinks that deep down inside everybody is essentially like him—or her. . . . Take, for example, men all think that deep down inside people are essentially men. [laughs] And women think that deep down inside, people are—or ought to be [laughs]—essentially women. Which is why men, say, after they've just made love with a woman will turn on the professional football game. People like football, you know. [laughs]." And it's also why women think that the only reason that anyone ever turns on professional football is to give offense [laughs]." When Blount gets back to the Jimmy the Greek episode after that interlude, he has prepared his audience to be more speculative than critical. He calls the Greek's racism "thigh envy" and points out that one could use the same combination of observation and skewed interpretation to indicate the existence of a "whole class of white people who have been bred to have short thighs so they'll stay put behind desks."

The key persona in Blount's stage humor is more than a Southerner-up-North; he is also The Poor Soul Who Must Explain Everything—to the generation before and after him. Blount is a rationalizer who is trying to define and justify a way to behave. "Roy Blount's Happy Hour and a Half" opens with his remarks on how parents of his generation have to explain sex to their children. He says, with reference to masturbation, that he was taught two things: "'Your body's a sacred temple,' and 'It's filthy, don't touch it.' But now parents—parents of my generation—not only have to give kids a better explanation than that, we have to explain to the next generation why they can't do it in a restaurant." In the stage show, Blount also draws on the essay "Whiskey," republished in *Now, Where Were We?*, to give one example of why certain Southern adults are different from their parents. Blount reaches back to the strict, teetotaling example of his mother to explain why he and his sister drink: "I think one reason Susan and I aren't dry, in our generation, is that we figured there was nothing we could do drunk ('You'll throw up on your party dress,' was one thing my mother told Susan) that could be as embarrassing as what my mother would do sober" (95).

Blount on stage does not face the severe limitations imposed by the TV talk-show format, for which long, subtle stage stories, enriched by asides, are reduced to ninety-second sound-bite anecdotes set up by questions from the host and sharp descriptions are usually lost in the drive for one-liner laughter. Blount's persona is not instantly telegenic; his appearance is ordinary, his attitude is subtle, and his mannerisms are not quirky enough to attract attention right away. Unlike other television appearances, in which he is asked to comment on the South or sports, the talk-show spots require that Blount be funny quickly. Though the appearances may be helpful to Blount as a way to try his humor and to increase book sales and lecture appointments, the humor is so attenuated that the literary quality is diminished. Fortunately, in the stage show Blount's type of extended humor has time to make, even though it is not the complete humor from the printed page. After the persona develops his relationship with the audience, flashes of the literary brilliance are allowed to show through. When acting out the role of a macho rooster, for instance, Blount can describe chickens running—"like monks holding up their cassocks"—in a quick phrase that does not break the mood or shift the persona too far toward fine talking.

Blount is more subdued and literary on the commercially available audiotapes, which are readings straight from the texts, in a studio with no audience. One set of audiotapes, published in 1983, includes readings from *Crackers* and *One Fell Soup* on one tape and an interview on another. On a second set, published simultaneously with *Now Where Were We?*, Blount reads twenty-four of the thirty-four selections.[20] The stage performances, done without a script, are more animated, and the tapes provided for this study indicate a basic set of stories.

Although most of the sketches in Blount's shows come from essays, some have preceded essays ("The Unbearable Lightness of Air Travel" in *Now, Where Were We?* started as a sketch in "Laugh at Lunch"). Two of his best "Happy Hour" sketches, both from his *Sports Illustrated* stories, and told with only slight variations in each show, were, in 1990, still incubating in the oral presentation. Each combines familiar elements: women, blacks, whites, and the contrast between sections of the country. Neither story can be done justice to by summary; each is a well-orchestrated ramble, a main story studded with anecdotes, with enough references to earlier stories to unify the performance.

The first story describes a trip to cover a Michigan football game, after which Blount attended a formal reception, drove to Detroit, and, with time on his hands before a flight departure, decided to see an adult movie, *Animal Lovers*. Describing the skid-row ticket seller reminds Blount of how much he looks like men who twist their hair in public libraries, which leads to an anecdote about an old white man in a Mississippi library who takes forever and a day to inquire of equally slow talking librarians about where he might order a piece of pie; the stalling frustrates a faster-talking general American, a young black woman who asks, at the conclusion of the exchange between white folks, where she can learn something about the army, because she wants to "get out of this damn town." The story demonstrates Blount's comic timing and what kind of Southern accent he does not have (for which the Northern audiences should be grateful). Returning to the main story, Blount works toward a climax that brings home his mother's sense of being constantly under surveillance (the point of the liquor-store anecdote told earlier). He is addressed "Hi, Roy" by the theater usher, who is described as even more sleazy than the ticket taker. Momentarily stunned, Blount discovers that he had forgotten to take off the "effusive" name tag pinned on him at the reception. The story prompts Blount to say that he would probably be recognized immediately in such a place now, since he has joined "the ranks of the vaguely, unsatisfyingly familiar-looking person," which sets up a story about his status at a celebrity golf tournament.

The second story is about Blount's coauthoring a feature with Wilt Chamberlain about the latter's retiring as "a dominant force" in professional basketball. The adventure ends up at Chamberlain's house in California, with Chamberlain so disturbed over the *Sports Illustrated* headline calling him "a" rather than "the" dominant force that he telephones New York to get it changed and is intimidated by a truly dominant, Bronx-accented white female switchboard operator at *Sports Illustrated*. The Chamberlain story gives Blount a chance to try out black voices and his version of the voice of Lily Tomlin's Ernestine. Most important, as a closing story it provides an opportunity for Blount to combine angles on race, gender, aging, manners, writing, sports, and, by implication, the South—in sum, the humorist's primary concerns. The show ends with the social and dramatic completeness of a comedy, humor worked toward the conclusion that people of all kinds—semibelligerent blacks and whites and one humorist—can get along in the world, despite differences that cannot be dismissed.

Underpinning Blount's stage humor is the primary persona drawn from his writing: The Person Who Would Embrace Every Definable Dichotomy. That character would be both Northern and Southern, male and female, black and white, prose writer and poet, genteel and coarse, single and married, traveler and homebody, rebel and patriot, liberal and conservative. Extracted from the prose and simplified, the stage persona explains how and where compromises and continuities can be found that allow such a person to live with the contrarieties of American life in the 1980s. The voice, as a reviewer said of the *Now, Where Were We?* persona, is "reassuringly subversive" with regard to political and social values.[21] "I have always tried to get as far to the left of center, politically, as I can without denying those of my instincts that might be called conservative, without losing aesthetic distance and without lapsing into cant," Blount said. "I feel heartened by liberal values, generally speaking, and threatened by reactionary values, always have, and I want to make readers feel respectively heartened and threatened by them too."[22]

Never able to accept only one side of any dichotomy, the comedian presumes to mirror the audience—a primary hurdle that Blount clears easily. But what he reflects is not merely divisiveness but also a longer, more unifying view of life than the typical wisecracking television comedian offers. However funny this literary humor may be, it is not trivial or mean-spirited. Partisan political criticism, even against Reagan, is subdued; about George Bush, Blount comments only on his inability to swear as creatively as Harry Truman or Lyndon Johnson. Although topical subjects crop up, Blount's literary humor is chiefly stories of childhood and travel, expressed through long, literary anecdotes that are meant to linger; the humor leaves the impression that the dichotomies *are* life, polestars for steering a way through stormy fin de siècle seas, and that the stories in which the dichotomies figure are too memorable to be dismissed. Without being maudlin or merely droll (the occasional expletive separates Blount from Bill Cosby), the literary comedian lets his stories build toward a conclusion: humor is a level for considering, possibly resolving, and certainly best living with important matters.

Chapter Eight
In His Own Humor: Lightest, Darkest, Latest

Is it just me, or does everything seem dumb in the eighties? So many movies, so many public utterances, so many people *buying* those movies and utterances.

Okay, my critics may say, so what have I been doing to make things better? Have I been forming a new political party? Have I been writing a major novel? Have I been serving as Secretary of Education?

No, I have been creating crossword puzzles. And I have been composing a double volume of verse that if you open it from one side is entitled *Soupsongs* and if you turn it over and open it from the other side is entitled *Webster's Ark.* Available in fine stores this month.

—Roy Blount, Jr., *Spy,* November 1987

A review of the principal writings of Roy Blount leaves the impression that he has taken as his province every perspective, subject, and audience in the country. The impression is hardly an illusion; in his exploration of American life Blount has, in fact, assumed a national as well as a Southern point of view, and he has used all of the media to express it. Moreover, in his bid to become the complete literary humorist, he has been anything but exclusive: from lost socks to talking wrenches, no subject is too mundane, and from androgyny to the presidency, none too forbidding. The democratic range of readers to whom his humor is addressed is evident in the publications in which it has appeared, a spectrum extending from the general readers of *Parade* and *TV Guide* to the middling intellectual readership of the *Atlantic* and the *New York Times Book Review.*

Within the several overlapping subsets that form Blount's entire audience is a smaller and more critical one, both metaphorical and real, which is probably the most demanding, most fun to play to, and least lucrative. Never defined explicitly, it manifests itself first as a voice, similar to the one Blount created in *Crackers,* that exists to keep the humorist on his toes. It tests the writing for authenticity, integrity, and logic; pushes the humorist to new inventions; checks silliness; and acts finally as the judge of what is funny. Yet the audience that is receptive to this display of the humorist's virtuosity is more than a rhetorical chorus. Corresponding to it is a real one, a smaller corps of readers and listeners, that represents the ethos of the humorist.

The implication of this audience within the writing, together with the attraction of readers and listeners who approximate it, is one of Roy Blount's major achievements. In his writing, this smaller and more critical audience is always played to and pulled against, humored and held at bay. Without forsaking the broader national audience, without appearing to be an elitist who tells esoteric inside jokes, Blount can at the same time (and often in the same essay) speak to readers capable of understanding, appreciating, and laughing at allusions, puns, and parodies. In Blount's humor the refined is always seeking the raw, and vice versa, a mutual need evident in the writing that extends to the audiences. If the appeal to the broad and the coarse appetites keeps the author from failing, as he said, in the direction of "primness," the presence of the higher audience prompts the humorist to stretch the primary persona, which is already such a direct extension of this higher audience that his playing to it often seems a form of self-address. How Blount uses that smaller audience as a check, a goad, and a sounding board is adumbrated in the humor in which he shows his lightest and his darkest sides, and in two forms less central to his popularity and less appealing to the broader audience—in the light verse and in the crossword puzzle-essays in *Spy* magazine.

What an audience receptive to light verse appreciates is the cleverness—the pure display of wit—that is possible when the humorist is frolicking with language, logic, literature, and society at large, using a playful form to demonstrate remarkable technical skill and knowledge. Dependent on the right mood and the right audience, Blount's light verse does not strive hard to be funny or profound; more demanding on the writer than on the reader, it is meant to amuse. Blount's light verse satisfies the definition set forth in Kingsley Amis's introduction to *The New Oxford Book of English Light Verse*—it is cheerful and lighthearted, but it is also "offensive to decorum," both to the formal standards of serious poetry and to social proprieties: "Unless engaged in parody, it prefers forms incompatible with decent seriousness: jogging rhythms, elaborate rhymes, stanzas that erect trip-wires for the unwary reader. It deals with low matters, subjects, scenes and concerns that are either poetically or morally unsuitable for high consideration. It uses low terms, whether rustic, technical, colloquial, facetiously anachronistic, or vulgar, ill-bred, obscene. Its chief weapon is impropriety."[1]

True to form, Blount's light verse resists analysis, even more so than the prose humor, and it requires little explication. His practice of the form extends to parodies, or "light verse proper," and popular verse, which does not play off serious poetry.[2] Whatever else it may be, Blount's light verse indicates that he is more than a commercial writer and that his range extends beyond the occasional essay.

As if to demonstrate that he meant to be the complete humorist, Blount began early to write light verse. In the anthology by E. B. and Katharine S. White (*A Subtreasury of American Humor*) that he pored over as a teenager, Blount saw that light verse was recognized as a popular form, one practiced by Dorothy Parker, Ogden Nash, and Don Marquis. As a columnist for the *Vanderbilt Hustler,* Blount found ways to slip in occasional verses, one of them the limerick that excludes the most obvious rhyme for *Aix.* His limericks in the *Atlanta Journal,* whose first lines used Georgia place names ("A girl of the Marshes of Glynn / Sank in them as well as in sin") were republished in *Crackers,* and one of the rhymes ("Bimini / chimini") was recovered for use in the "Prairie Home Companion" valedictory, "Good and Over." The poem about the ballet dancer named Sleep who crossed and uncrossed his legs five times in a single leap ("For the Record") appeared in the *New Yorker* while Blount was a staff writer for *Sports Illustrated* and was reprinted at the conclusion of *One Fell Soup.* For the most part, however, Blount's light verse has been sprinkled throughout the essays and generally overshadowed by the prose humor. Often it appears to provide tonal transitions or visual relief within or between prose pieces; however, such an impression belies the importance of light verse in Blount's repertoire. In an essay of assorted notes published in *Antaeus* in 1988, Blount offers a free-verse defense of his poetry, which reads in part:

> Here's a clean breast of it:
> I think I am not fine enough
> For the Beloit Poetry Journal.
> Which I've never seen an issue of!
> Where the fuck is Beloit! I
> Had a poem in *The New Yorker!*

> "Light verse," demurmurs the Muse. [Blount's period.]
> "Rhymes." Why is it that some people's Muses
> Bear them aloft and mine is always
> Clearing her throat?
> I wouldn't mind a Muse that eluded me;
> Mine can be had but has
> A faraway look in her eye.[3]

Country music lyrics, which reinforce the grass-roots persona, were Blount's most common early form of light verse. The best display of it is in "Whiskey and Blood" in *Crackers,* an essay praising country music, specifically lyrics of the kind written by Billy Joe Shaver, which put to music *"the way people put things"* (144). Blount demonstrates his own ability to write parodies of songs that seem self-parodying, yet do so in a way that honors rather than mocks the form. He reaches for literary allusions, imagining that he is Buddy Roe Bear and His Ruined Choir singing, as Walt Whitman might:

> His *life* was a *mix*ture of *great* rights and *wrongs.*
> He wrote *bad* checks, his *ma*ma and *beau*tiful *songs.*
> He *lived* in the *pines* with the *great* speckled *bird.*
> He *wrote* every *tune* and he *earned* every *word.* (144)

Blount's social-comment song, "It's a Coldhearted World," is less a parody of country music than it is of sixties protest songs, of the windmills-of-the-mind variety sung by Bob Dylan, Joan Baez, and the Beatles. It opens:

> Everything real is vinyl,
> Everything vinyl is real,
> Everything temporary's final,
> Everything final will heal.
> Every little bend is straightened,
> Everything straight is curled—
> When the mannikins have nipples
> It's a coldhearted world.

And it closes, "When pinup girls got pubic hair, it's a coldhearted world" (156–157). In the stage appearances, Blount can evoke parody merely by citing the title of a song he has written: "You Know How a

Dog's Leg Twitches When You Scratch Him on the Belly, Well That
Is How My Heart Is Beating Darlin' over You."

By the mid-1980s, Blount's light verse was making its way into
anthologies, among them four issues of the *Light Year* annuals. ("Song
against Broccoli" was also included in two British anthologies.)[4] Generally, a poem in the Blount mode introduces literary figures into unlikely settings, as he often does in the prose—for instance, by
imagining Henry Adams as a football coach in *About Three Bricks Shy
of a Load* and Walt Whitman as a sportswriter in *What Men Don't Tell
Women.* In "Gutes and Eulas," which consists of twelve six-line stanzas,
wits are matched between unlikely historical and literary couples—
Gutenberg and Eula Snopes, Scheherezade and Billy the Kid, Don Juan
and Nurse Sue Barton, Mickey Spillane and Guinevere, Gypsy Rose
Lee and Jack the Ripper, Becky Sharp and Samuel Johnson, Mary Pop-
pins and Genghis Khan, Job and *la belle dame sans merci,* Lee Harvey
Oswald and Lady Macbeth, *la belle dame* and the Marquis de Sade,
Frank Sinatra and Molly Bloom, and Friedrich Nietzsche and Lois
Lane. The winning riposte is saved for the final couplet of each stanza:

> When Gutenberg met Eula Snopes
> She raised in him unprintable hopes.
> But very soon he ran aground
> Upon her earthiness profound.
>   "You're not for me, although you're ripe,"
>   Said G.: "I like the moveable type."

Who will get the last word creates the suspense:

> When Frank Sinatra met Molly Bloom,
> He sang mellow, filled the room.
> Yes she said Yes. He sang smooth and low.
> Yes she said Yes. He sang My Way. No
>   She said: Sure I'm willing to go along
>   But that she said is a terrible song.[5]

The publication of *Soupsongs/Webster's Ark* in 1987 put Blount's light
verse in its own showcase. The book is actually two fifty-five-page
collections of light verse, bound back to back and upside down, each
with its own cover and each illustrated with antique black-and-white
line drawings, a format clever enough in itself to attract attention. The

forty-two poems in *Soupsongs*—all dealing with some aspect of food—begin with a paean to eating and conclude with a tribute to the poet's stomach. In between are verses to ham, broccoli, green peas, okra, oysters, gumbo, open-air cooking, beans, chicken, grits, the apple, bacon, onions, hamburgers, hot dogs, covered dishes, butter, the "patata," grease, the lentil, legumes in general, homemade ice cream, drink, pizza, pie, catfish, eggs, ribs, beef, cobbler, catsup, barbecue sauce, beets, chitlins, rice, peaches, watermelon, health food, and the tomato. Fourteen of the poems first appeared as a unit in *One Fell Soup*, in a grouping of seventeen poems under the title "A Near Score of Food Songs." The two-line Nashian verse, "The neighborhood stores are all out of broccoli / Loccoli," for which Blount received praise in the reviews of *Soupsongs/Webster's Ark*, went virtually unrecognized when buried deep in the first prose collection (*One Fell Soup*, 57; *Soupsongs/Webster's Ark*, 6).

As the food choices indicate, *Soupsongs* tilts southward. About grits, for instance, Blount writes:

> When my mind's unsettled,
> When I don't feel spruce,
> When my nerves get frazzled,
> When my flesh gets loose,
> What knits
> Me back together's grits. (16)

The poet also prefers "a nice girl and dish of okra" to "strip pokra":

> It may be poor for eating chips with,
> It may be hard to come to grips with,
> But okra's such a whole food,
> It straightens out your attitude. (9)

Turning to the universals, in "Song to Catsup," addressed to "young and particular readers," Blount shows how much fun the light verse poet can have with language:

> If every food your parents hatsup
> Tastes like something to matsup
> With something not even a buzzard would snatsup,
> Add catsup. (42)

What the poet says about insipid supermarket tomatoes in "Song to
Love Apples," however, is more earnest editorial opinion than clown-
ing around:

> They are no more tomatoes
> Than the Rev. Norman Vincent Peale,
> Who wrote *The Power of Positive Thinking,*
> Is the Rev. Jonathan Edwards,
> Who wrote *Sinners in the Hands of an Angry God.*
> You don't have to think positively about a tomato.
> You get caught up in it.

Of the store-bought tomatoes, whose fathers were "neoprene lemons"
and which Blount calls "celluloid things" that merely ship well, he
says,

> They've spent more time being transported
> Than getting good. Like bland
> Quasi-mystical young rich girls,
> Who've been humped all over Europe
> And in and out of finishing schools,
> But never got well enough started.

On the other hand, true "love apples," from a garden plot, a roadside
stand, or a farmer's market get another comparison:

> *Real* tomatoes I would compare
> To a lover's mouth. Take them
> Round and warm from the sun
> As her round shoulder. (52–53)

Webster's Ark, Blount's alphabetic bestiary and herbal, moves
through forty-five poems, from aardvark to zygote, through such obscure animals as the cacomistle and cassowary and such plants as hen-
bane and ylang-ylang. Setting off on his journey, the poet advises the
reader to

> Look up! Clouds of roots and owls
> Rain down consonants and vowels,
> Enzymes, pottos, worts in ferment!
> And viscerally I'm dèterment

> As a beaver to debark.
> We're off! (see the aardvark?) Off on an ark!
> No, I don't have all the answers.
> But I do have all these stanzas. (1)

The poems are untitled (though the subjects are set in all-uppercase boldface), most are short, and the wit in them often turns on spelling puns, line breaks, and parodic allusions intended to elicit groans, guffaws, and an admiration for the poet's metrical cleverness. Of the chamois, for instance, Blount writes:

> We were singing "Mamois"
> And a little bit of "Tamois
> 's in Love" and "Alabamois
> Bound"—hey hey—
>
> And a gal there who was gamois
> And anything but clamois
> Said we should win a Gramois,
> Singing that way.
>
> She sidled up to Samois,
> Winked at him and, whamois,
> Said, "Rub me, big chamois,
> You know the way." (12)

Of a prickly anteater he writes,

> What if, to test your poise as lovers,
> Someone had hidna
> Spiny-coated, slender-snouted, burrowing ECHIDNA
> In your and your loved one's covers? (18)

Usually a parodist in passing allusions ("Some rough yeast . . . "), the poet draws on famous lines from *The Tempest* in a couplet to match the broccoli poem from *Soupsongs*: "Where the COWSLIP / There slip I" (16). The poem to the zygote, one of the longest in *Webster's Ark,* both concludes the collection and describes the format of the book. Explaining that he himself started out "zygotic" but wound up "incomplete, neurotic," the poet traces the sperm's longing for the egg and of human beings' desire to return to the zygote:

> But if we got there, we wouldn't stay long,
> There is no end to the zygote song.
> And no place to turn to answer the riddle:
> *It comes from the end and meets in the middle.* (55)

The collections did not strike all reviewers as funny. Daniel Pink-water in a short notice in the *New York Times Book Review* said the "cute verses" that "may have given pleasure" when published alone "turn into a surfeit when strung together." He did not like the Southern slant of *Soupsongs,* calling Blount a "Gourmet Rube," but he did have a kind word for the "Zen simplicity" of *Webster's Ark.*[6] (Blount answered Pink-water in one of his final "Happy Hour and a Half" presentations by poking fun at the reviewer's name.) Typically, however, the reviews were favorable and, equally typically, full of comparisons—with Ogden Nash, mainly, but at least once with Shel Silverstein.[7] Some reviews appearing before Christmas 1987 mentioned the book as an ideal gift. Wayne Greenhaw, writing in the *Montgomery Advertiser and Alabama Journal,* said Blount "may be the funniest writer in the United States today," and Frank Gannon, also a Southern literary humorist (author of *Yo, Poe!* and *Vanna Karenina*), reviewing in the Atlanta papers, wrote that with the publication of the light verse "Blount finally fulfills the entrance requirement for the Renaissance man's club."[8]

Not all of Blount's verse outside the collections can be called light; some reflects his graver concerns with the eighties and the attitudes he associates with Reaganism. In "A Christmas Carol (for the 80's)," a sixty-four-line poem that ran on the op-ed page of the *New York Times* in December 1988, Blount sees Scrooge's conversion as the beginning of the commercialization of Christmas that yielded, among other things, the "coffee-table book" and evergreen farming; the acceptance of Scrooge's conversion replaced "the urge to be retentive" with "*incentive.*" The United States, the poem contends, is in "Scrooge's debt," but he "will have to wait in line," for the country, which owes "billions to ourselves and other countries," has become a "wealthy moocher." Christmas Future does not "haunt us like the spectre of it old Scrooge saw," because abstract fiscal policies are a newest Scrooge, preying on the poor. The poem ends with a rhetorical question:

> If we owe too many dollars, why we'll lower
> The dollar's value, and pinch some more

Pennies from the Federal budget shares
Of those who live on prayers.
Or so it looks from here, and who am I to say
That conceivably the way
It looks from heaven sickens
Dickens?[9]

Much of the humor that is animated by Blount's discontent with the attitudes of the 1980s appears in the crossword puzzles he began to write in October 1986 for *Spy,* which he describes as "basically a smart-ass monthly, which makes fun of the rich and successful (unusual for the Eighties)."[10] In the 1989 edition of *Writer's Market,* the periodical is defined as "a non-fiction satirical magazine published ten times a year," with a circulation listed at sixty-five-thousand.[11] The crossword form itself is Blount's response to British puzzles based on the most obscure trivia: "The way some Americans watch *The Young and the Restless,* I need to work the preposterously cryptic crosswords developed in the London *Times.* I do not need, however, to be stumped by towns in Sussex, horticultural terms peculiar to the Twittage and cricket references. . . . I want an American puzzle that says, 'In your face, Britannia! Never listened to the Five Satins, did you, Mrs. Thatcher? And what does a developed country need with princes and princesses?'"[12]

Though there apparently are readers witty enough and close enough to Blount's wavelength actually to work the "un-British" puzzles, the clues are mainly a device for the author's explanation of the answers. For instance, in the September 1987 puzzle—subheaded the "Sexism and Depravity Special"—the clue for an eight-letter word is, "Will Gary Hart ever again do a Christine Jorgenson?" The answer is "womanize," and Blount explains,

Do a Christine Jorgenson (she was the first man to achieve fame by becoming a woman) alone, with all due respect and the double meaning of *do,* would have done here. But this puzzle, this month, is not about to err on the side of simple elegance. And we got to have Hart. To ask *Will Gary Hart ever again?* is to imply an almost misty-eyed compassion for the man—a measure of the depths to which this puzzle descends. Put yourself in his shoes, though. Which reminds me that someone once said of Warren Beatty, "He puts his pants on one leg at a time just like everybody else. He just does it more often."[13]

Within a year, Blount had two full pages for his *Spy* humor, one for the puzzle and another for his answers, which included an introductory essay and, as he had promised at the start, "notes for readers who think that this effort, like 'The Wasteland,' is a load of Anglo-American rubbish." The puzzle answers often include excerpts from earlier essays, snippets from stage presentations, or bits of light verse already published; they are also apparently a first draft of ideas to be treated later. The introductions and the thematically ordered "answers" are prime for shaping into full essays.

Progressively, as the 1988 presidential election neared, the humor grew more political, less circumspect, and more vituperative. In the November 1987 puzzle, Blount explains why "fictional" is the answer to the clue, "Novel quality of president's character":

Being fictional is a quality of a novel. And fictionality is the key to Ronald Reagan's character. He is a figment of his audience's imagination. If the audience is Ollie North, Reagan offers the laddie-buck sly but unmistakable encouragement. If the audience is George Shultz, Reagan looks "as if he'd been kicked in the stomach" when Shultz tells him what North has been up to. If the audience is Tip O'Neill, Reagan is a dumber chief executive than would have been imaginable. And all these characters *play*. When the camera rules, the question is not whether you add up but whether you *work*. This accounts for how Reagan has been so clever and so vapid, both: clever enough to ingratiate himself multifariously and vapid enough to believe in himself, himself. No wonder he tells so many Errol Flynn stories.[14]

In August 1988, Blount devoted most of the puzzle to the Reagan administration, taking shots particularly at the president for allowing his press secretary to fabricate remarks for him:

I keep trying to figure out whether I have no sense of objective reality at all or Ronald Reagan is in fact president. I am thinking of writing a story in which a man decides, "If Ronald Reagan is president, then I am not real." A feeling of peace comes over him. He stops keeping up with the news. Hence diminished role of government in his life. Paradoxically, he becomes more real. Then one Sunday evening he comes home from a carefree weekend trip with his family, hears funny noises out back, finds Ed Meese [attorney general in the Reagan administration] in his IF YOU CAN'T STAND THE HEAT apron, cooking steaks on his grill.[15]

The next month, he said Reagan was "an innocence machine" and a "national drug" until he *"finally* wore thin."[16]

In Blount's humor Reagan is inevitably associated with the eighties, with a decline in concern for human welfare, with greed and selfishness, and with the necessity of humor. In the *Spy* issue that appeared the month of the presidential election, Blount connects Reagan, George Bush, and the general attitudes of the decade: " 'I've gotten immune to criticism,' George Bush says. All right, one can see that. But isn't there, among the general, sane population, a growing sense that immunity is not what it used to be? In the 1980s, Ronald Reagan has undoubtedly served an enormous prophylactic function, but don't you get an inkling every now and then that if a mainstream eighties American *could* catch malaise, this is how it would feel?" Blount establishes a connection between Bush's remark and the disease of the decade, AIDS, which attacks the autoimmune system, and he presses the metaphor: "[Y]ou proceed to the beach (wearing, even in autumn, six-power sunblock just to give yourself the same level of protection against carcinogenic solar radiation that the ozone layer used to provide) and a used hypodermic needle comes in with the tide." In the same issue, Blount acknowledges how good the eighties have been to one who earns his "bread by tickling America's funny bone" and asks if an "appreciation of the irony of the situation ever *stopped* making the nation feel charmed, where would that leave guys like me?"[17]

The change in administration, however, did not improve Blount's disposition, which drifted more and more toward a rancor barely concealed by the humor in the crossword answers. A visceral and philosophical disgruntlement with the age pervades the *Spy* writings, though it is rarely the primary stuff of the humor. In the March 1989 issue, Blount identifies himself as a liberal Democrat who did not vote for George Bush, as a Southerner with a bias against conservatives, and as a writer in agreement with George Will, who called Bush a "lapdog." At the end of the answers, a comment about aerobics and the age suddenly shifts in tone to resume the theme: "Liberals have got to get *vigorous* again. I'll tell you this: I voted for Dukakis, but I'm not going to go out walking with Heavy Hands."[18]

In the months following Bush's election, Blount began a steady assault on the decade that was nearing its end. He saw the manipulation of money as the index of the age, and his vision of the direction of the country was too dark to allow for much humor. In the February 1989 issue of *Spy,* he explains why people look up answers to puzzles without trying to work out the answers themselves: "I do not condemn you. I lay it all on the doorstep of Ronald Wilson Reagan, who throughout the eighties has been so at home in his own skin, wattles and all, that who among the rest of us have not felt, deep down inside, just a leetle bit jittery in comparison? It seems to me only fair, at the close of the Reagan years, that *every American* be provided a nice underpriced Bel Air estate to retire to."[19] In the March 1989 issue, he says why he does not feel at home in the eighties: "What the eighties keeps doing is drawing another advance. I blame it on the Japanese—when they introduced sushi over here and Americans developed a taste for those little raw dabs of marine life, it broke down the age-old taboo against eating your bait. After a while, what have you got left to fish with?"[20] In the April 1989 issue, he reveals why *risk* is the answer to the clue, "Prudent person lends to these or takes them": "Hard to say what constitutes a good risk in the eighties. The "thrifts—such down-to-earth-home financing institutions as the building-and-loan glorified in *It's A Wonderful Life*—are sucking wind. Treasury bills have nothing behind them but the U.S. government. And what with LBOs [leveraged buy outs] and junk bonds and all, who knows what collateral is anymore?"[21]

In May 1989, in a puzzle subtitled "Charity and the Bottom Line," Blount sees the government as an extension of the selfishness of citizens: "I don't do anything for the wretched unless they are thrust upon me and the odds are that neither do you. It has always seemed to me that the best way of thrusting the wretched upon the rest of us (riots aside) is taxes, imposed by a government that is willing to *represent* people who are suffering and dying. Such a notion is, of course, utterly out of date. It just doesn't add up."[22] In the June 1989 puzzle, following an explanation that "death rattle" is a "final noise," he tries to soften the tone: "Here's a day of reckoning question for you: are the "We're Number One" eighties in fact, for America, a terminal loud empty noise? No, I don't think so. It is just that the eighties have given self-esteem a bad name. In the seventies, self-esteem's name was Muhammad Ali; in the eighties, Donald Trump. In the nineties, you never know, it might be someone who works crossword puzzles."[23] In the July 1989 puzzle, in one of his sharpest criticisms, Blount sees the new administration epitomized in Republican National Chairman Lee Atwater, who plays blues with black musicians: "As we all know, the eighties, generally speaking, have developed differently [from the seventies]. The predominant vandals have been waves of *Republicans* unable—or rather, not required—to tell right from wrong, Republicans determined to take in all Americans, white and black, who have any money at all."[24]

The sharp political views expressed in *Spy* reappear in the novel *First Hubby,* begun in 1983 and published in June 1990. The narrator, Guy Fox, a humorist, is the husband of the first woman president of the United States, who succeeds from the vice presidency after the incumbent is killed by a falling fish. The comic situation provides more platform than plot; isolated by political events, sex, and age, the narrator reflects on the nation, the past, and his own life, which resembles Blount's. Unlike Blount, Fox has had only one wife, the ideal modern woman. Lonely, if not lost, Fox writes a diary that moves from the present to the past, especially to his happier times as a journalist, a lover, and, most especially, a father. When he speaks of his daughter and son, now grown and away from home, Fox openly grieves: "It's as if there were a rope of heart, a cardiac rope, between me and them and on one end it still pulls as hard on me, and oh, I know it probably pulls on them, nostalgically at least, at their end, but between us these days, there is a slack, a missingness, that somehow or other, can't be taken up"(83). Fox's melancholia sets *First Hubby* apart from other Blount works; beneath the political intelligence, the puns, the inside jokes, and the vernacular humor lies more than the anxiety of the Man Who Must Explain Everything. In *First Hubby,* Blount faces the mortality of his generation and imagines a resurrection, never denying that the America envisioned in the novel is, like the narrator, an array of remnants that can be drawn together as a source of darkening humor but not into a coherent pattern for entering a new century. Typically, the humorist makes his point, then leaves for other territory.

Anyone who looks at the fullness of Blount's career through his first forty-nine years will be aware of how he has, like Mark Twain, appropriated so many of the traditions of American humor and presented them in such a range of forms to so broad an audience. He has been, by turns and sometimes simultaneously, a reporter, an editorialist, a columnist, a sportswriter, an essayist, a literary comedian, a light verse poet, a novelist, and a political commentator. He has demonstrated a remarkable independence for a man dependent on his wits in an open market, not selling his talent where it could make the most money, seeking out the audiences that force him to sharpen his humor, and always holding to his ideal.

It is apparent from a study of Roy Blount's career that he has always had a vision of himself as humorist and, with that vision, a sense of how humor goes to the heart of basic conflicts, defines those conflicts on its own terms, and takes a step toward reconciling them. Whatever the "level of humor" is, Blount knows where it is, and in matters large and small, he finds it. His humor pleases because it illuminates life as all good literature does. In Blount's world, nothing is too mean to sparkle with humor, and nothing is too lofty to be approachable.

Whether Roy Blount, Jr., ever attains the stature of Robert Benchley or Mark Twain is less important than what he has already done. What can be said about his literary humor now is that he appears well on his way to being like other great American humorists and, like them, of sufficient stature to be a standard of comparison. His writing and performance already reveal the mysterious genius of humor generally; furthermore, through his sharp insight into the nature of the country, his affection for the nation, and his keen literary and historical sense, his writing confirms for his generation of readers the validity and the value of humor.

More like Walt Whitman than Mark Twain in his ambition, Blount has attempted to embrace all American audiences and, in his own way, to humor and cheer the country, for at the heart of his humor is the realization that the country needs to be humored. In an introduction to the republication of A. J. Liebling's *The Telephone Booth Indian*, Blount recalls being home from graduate school at Christmas 1963 and telling his parents he wanted to be like "this fat Jewish man," rather than an English professor; a quarter-century later he still wants to be like the *New Yorker* humorist.[25] Even in "the hollowly booming eighties," which Blount considers a time "of underclass, crack, postmodernism, Big Numbers, cartoonishness, and consuming Republicanism," such a humorist is needed to elevate the human spirit. Using Liebling as a benchmark, Roy Blount, Jr., restates his ambition: "[H]ere's something that I think funny writers do, in America at least: they reprise over and over the struggle up through big *d* or little *d* depression, they're fascinated by it, they *get down* in that sense, and they keep coming up as long as they can. It's not an ignoble struggle, and I hope to hell I can leave behind some stuff that makes people's hearts jump half so high."

Notes and References

Chapter One

1. For a clear explanation of the major theories of humor, see Norman Holland, *Laughing: A Psychology of Humor* (Ithaca, N.Y., and London: Cornell University Press, 1982).
2. "What's So Humorous?," in *Not Exactly What I Had in Mind* (New York: Penguin Books, 1985), 174–75.
3. Aristotle, *The "Art" of Rhetoric,* trans. John Henry Freeze (Cambridge, Mass.: Harvard University Press; and London: Heinemann, 1959), 251.
4. E. B. White and Katharine S. White, *A Subtreasury of American Humor* (New York: Coward-McCann, 1941), xvii.
5. Joseph Epstein, "Sid, You Made the Prose Too Thin," *Commentary* 84 (September 1987):60.

Chapter Two

1. Letter to author, 13 October 1988.
2. Ibid.
3. [Unsigned obituary], "Roy A. Blount: S & L President," *Atlanta Constitution,* 17 April 1974, 14-A.
4. [Unsigned], "Blount Ends Term with Press Blast," *Atlanta Constitution,* 29 December 1972, 18-A.
5. Ibid.
6. [Unsigned editorial], "Roy A. Blount, Sr." *Atlanta Constitution,* 18 April 1974, 4-A.
7. *Crackers* (New York: Knopf, 1980), 260.
8. Phil Kloer, "The Blount Truth," *Atlanta Weekly,* 29 March 1987, 12.
9. Daniel Penrice, "Blount-edged Humor," *Boston Globe Sunday Magazine,* 17 June 1984, 35.
10. "How Miss Wren Stood in De Do'," in *One Fell Soup* (Boston: Little, Brown, 1982), 90–92.
11. Letter to author, 31 May 1989.
12. Susan Blount, telephone conversation with author, 27 March 1989.
13. Letter to author, 31 May 1989.
14. Carson J. Robison, "Life Gits Tee-jus, Don't It," in *Sing Your Heart*

Out, Country Boy, ed. Dorothy Horstman (Nashville, Tenn.: Country Music Foundation, 1986), 110–11. Lyrics vary in the recorded versions.

15. Letter to author, 18 July 1989.

16. Susan Blount, telephone conversation with author, 27 March 1989.

17. "Roy (Alton) Blount, Jr.," in *Contemporary Authors New Revision Series,* vol. 10 (Detroit, Mich.: Gale Research, 1983), 54.

18. Blount to Charles J. Cella, 14 March 1986, Special Collections, Jean and Alexander Heard Library, Vanderbilt University, Nashville, Tennessee.

19. *One Fell Soup,* ix.

20. Blount to Charles J. Cella, 14 March 1986.

21. Letter to author, 13 October 1988.

22. "Chancellor's Chapel Talk Asks Proper Breadth in Education," *Vanderbilt Hustler,* 2 October 1959, 1.

23. "Senate Endorses Oust of Lawson Unanimously, Passes New Constitution," *Vanderbilt Hustler,* 11 March 1960, 1.

24. "'No Position' Taken on Yates by 'V,'" *Vanderbilt Hustler,* 15 April 1960, 1.

25. [Unsigned], "Alexander V-Book Head; Blount Is Associate Editor," *Vanderbilt Hustler,* 21 April 1961, 1.

26. "VU Students Have Access to Coffee House Atmosphere (18 Kinds) at Tulip Is Black,'" *Vanderbilt Hustler,* 30 September 1960, 1.

27. "VU Humor Magazine Has Long, Unhappy Past," *Vanderbilt Hustler,* 3 March 1961, 1.

28. [Unsigned], "Editor Daughtrey Promises Humor in Next Year's 'Vagabond' Issues," *Vanderbilt Hustler,* 12 May 1961, 1.

29. "Porter Reads 'Jilting,' Warren Speaks to Highlight VU Literary Symposium," *Vanderbilt Hustler,* 28 April 1961, 1.

30. "John Crowe Ransom to Return Next Fall," *Vanderbilt Hustler,* 10 February 1961, 1.

31. "Out with Curry, in with Law School; Squirrel Water Situation Called Critical," *Vanderbilt Hustler,* 19 May 1961, 1.

32. "Alexander V-Book Head," *Hustler,* 1.

33. Lamar Alexander, "Blount 'Rumbles' His Way through Hilarious Book," *Nashville Banner,* 8 April 1989, D-10.

34. "John Crowe Ransom 'at Home with Everybody,' to Close Out Teaching Career after Long Absence," *Vanderbilt Hustler,* 29 September 1961, 1.

35. "Stabbing, Pizza Mark Ride with Police," *Vanderbilt Hustler,* 8 December 1961, 1.

36. Diane Monk, "'Regenerated' Vagabond to Have Balance of Humor, Prose, Poetry," *Vanderbilt Hustler,* 16 February 1962, 5.

37. "Enter Sanders, with a Few Words on Conservatism, and Coed Shorts," *Vanderbilt Hustler,* 10 November 1961, 4.

38. "We're Nice, Normal Enough; No Twirlers in Slacks Needed," *Vanderbilt Hustler,* 29 September 1961, 4.

39. "There's Not Any Bunk in UGF, Says the 32-inch Poem of Mr. S," *Vanderbilt Hustler,* 3 November 1961, 4.

40. "'Male Animal' Does for Professors What Even 'Seminar Six' Wouldn't," *Vanderbilt Hustler,* 20 October 1961, 4.

41. "Touchy Composition in Black and White," *Vanderbilt Hustler,* 12 January 1962, 4.

42. Blount, "Of Time and Place, and Smugness of Race," *Vanderbilt Hustler,* 20 April 1962, 4.

43. "On Intellectual Climate, and Bettering It," *Vanderbilt Hustler,* 2 March 1962, 5.

44. Jim Foster, "ODK Taps Six Junior Leaders," *Vanderbilt Hustler,* 18 May 1962, 1.

45. "Of Chancellor, Bias, Art, Laughter, Aix," *Vanderbilt Hustler,* 11 May 1962, 4.

46. "Maria Beale Fletcher Wants to Forget Miss America and 'Just Be Me,'" *Vanderbilt Hustler,* 14 September 1962, 1.

47. "Coolidge on Rush: 'Don't,'" *Vanderbilt Hustler,* 28 September 1962, 4.

48. "The Sound of Music," *Vanderbilt Hustler,* 14 September 1962, 4.

49. "Prospectus," *Vanderbilt Hustler,* 14 September 1962, 4.

50. "The Silent Senate," *Vanderbilt Hustler,* 12 October 1962, 4.

51. Lionel Barrett, "Senate President Breaks Silence, Hits 'H' Misconception, Typos,'" *Vanderbilt Hustler,* 19 October 1962, 5.

52. "Arguing and the Senate," *Vanderbilt Hustler,* 19 October 1962, 4.

53. "South Forgets Its Own Values," *Vanderbilt Hustler,* 19 October 1962, 4.

54. "More Attorney and Less General," *Vanderbilt Hustler,* 30 November 1962, 4.

55. "Some of Our Best Friends," *Vanderbilt Hustler,* 7 December 1962, 4.

56. [Unsigned], "Hustler, Other College Publications Explode in Nationwide Headlines," *Vanderbilt Hustler,* 3 May 1963), 2.

57. John M. Aden, "Professors, Students Comment on Sit-in Controversy," *Vanderbilt Hustler,* 11 January 1963, 10.

58. Blount, "Two Alums and Their Different Books," *Vanderbilt Hustler,* 26 April 1963, 4.

59. "Compare Agrarians, Black Power," *Atlanta Journal,* 7 May 1968, 17-A; "Davidson: Whole in His Acts," *Atlanta Journal,* 9 May 1968, 21-A.

60. "Is Your Daddy Greek?" *Vanderbilt Hustler,* 15 February 1963, 4.

61. "Frozen Leopard: Hemingway and the Code," *Spectrum* 1 (Fall 1962):22–28.

62. "Adrift in a School of Sharks and Other Uneasy Circumstances," *Spectrum* 1 (Spring 1963):47–49.

63. "You Can't Go Home Again," *Vanderbilt Hustler,* 16 November 1962, 4.

64. "Shaw and Comedy—Fire and Ice and Some Interesting Things in Between," *Spectrum* 2 (Fall 1963):28–34.

65. Susan Blount, telephone conversation with author, 27 March 1989.

66. *Crackers,* 80.

67. Ibid., 81.

68. Letter to author, 13 October 1988.

69. Kim Chapin, "Under Sharp Lens of a Native Son, Carter Falls Short," *Atlanta Journal-Constitution,* 9 November 1980, 2-E.

70. Personnel files, *Atlanta Journal-Constitution,* Atlanta, Georgia.

71. Letter to author, 13 October 1988.

72. Ibid.

73. Unless otherwise indicated, information on the *Atlanta Journal* and Blount's days as editorial writer is from a telephone interview with Reese Cleghorn conducted 5 April 1989.

74. "With Reservations, in Reserve," *Atlanta Journal,* 22 June 1967, 15-B.

75. "Ours Is Just to Reason Why," *Atlanta Journal,* 19 December 1967, 15-A.

76. "You Wouldn't Say 'Nigroo Power,'" *Atlanta Journal,* 29 February 1968, 23-A.

77. "Whatever Happened to Socks?," *Atlanta Journal,* 12 July 1967, 17-B; "The Socks Problem," in *One Fell Soup,* 35–37.

78. *Crackers,* 56.

79. Telephone conversation with author, 18 May 1989. All information about Blount's teaching is drawn from this conversation.

80. Cleghorn, telephone conversation with author, 5 April 1989.

81. The two *Crackers* essays cited in this paragraph are entitled "Yazoo" and "Being from Georgia."

82. Letter to author, 13 October 1988.

83. "A Paper Tiger Wins with Steel," *Sports Illustrated,* 5 August 1968, 46–48.

84. Letter to author, 13 October 1988.

85. "The Big Zinger from Binger," *Sports Illustrated,* 31 March 1969, 27.

86. Ibid., 34.

87. "A New Slant on an Old Game in Atlanta," *Sports Illustrated,* 1 September 1969, 40.

88. Ibid.

89. Letter to author, 31 May 1989.

90. Letter to author, 13 October 1988.

91. "A Torrid Time for the Twins," *Sports Illustrated,* 21 July 1969, 16.

92. "Yo Yo Yo, Rowa Hu Rowa, Hru Hru," *Sports Illustrated,* 7 April 1972, 50.

93. "I'm the Type of Swimmer Lifeguards Hate," *Sports Illustrated,* 18 June 1973, 36.

94. "Knock 'Im Out, Jay-ree!" *Sports Illustrated,* 30 April 1973, 83.

95. Ibid., 75.

96. Letter to author, 13 October 1988.

97. "Guess Who's Coming Up Now," *Sports Illustrated,* 23 June 1969, 50.

98. [Noah Sanders, pseud.], "Pistol Pete Is up against the Pros," *New York Times Magazine,* 11 October 1970, 32–33, 130-36; [C.R. Ways, pseud.], "'Nobody Does Anything Better Than Me in Baseball,' Says Roberto Clemente . . . Well, He's Right," *New York Times Magazine,* 9 April 1972, 38.

99. Letter to author, 20 May 1989.

100. Letter to author, 13 October 1988.

101. "For the Record," *New Yorker,* 29 April 1974, 42.

102. Letter to author, 13 October 1988.

103. "Who's Who in the Cast," *Playbill,* February 1988, 34. The "piranha attack" to which Blount refers is the subject of one of his most popular anecdotes. It comes from "Attacking the Amazon," *Sports Illustrated,* 13 April 1987, 60. A longer version of this story of the trip he and his son took to Amazonian Peru is "Amazon Adventure," in *Paths Less Travelled,* ed. Richard Bangs and Christian Kallen (New York: Atheneum, 1988), 131–46.

104. Letter to author, 13 October 1988.

Chapter Three

1. Except where otherwise noted, information and direct quotations on Blount's career as a free-lance humorist come from three letters to the author, 20 May 1989, 31 May 1989, and 17 July 1989, and from telephone conversations with Roy Blount, Susan Blount, and Joan Ackermann-Blount.

2. Richard Rosen, "Heirs to Maxwell Perkins," *Horizon,* April 1981, 52. The story to which Blount refers ran without a byline. "A New Look for the Old Ball Game," *Time,* 26 April 1976, 70.

3. "For the Record," *New Yorker,* 29 April 1974, 42.

4. "Whose Who?," *New Yorker,* 14 August 1978, 28–29; reprinted in *One Fell Soup,* 98–103.

5. Rosen, "Heirs to Maxwell Perkins," 52.

6. *"Esquire's* Irksome Quirks," *Columbia Journalism Review* 21 (September/October 1982):16; "A Blount Reply," *Pittsburgh Post-Gazette,* 11 September 1982, 6.

7. Ibid. Blount does not mention Touchett by name in "Why Wayne Newton's Is Bigger Than Yours," his essay on money, first published in *Playboy* in February 1983 and reprinted in *What Men Don't Tell Women:* "'Money,' says a character in *Portrait of a Lady,* 'is a terrible thing to follow but a charming thing to meet.' Might as well acknowledge it the way you do death, guilt, excreta, etcetera" (105).

8. Blount wrote about the experience in "Adventures in the Demme Monde," *Esquire,* September 1988, 207.

Chapter Four

1. References are to the Ballantine Books paperback (New York, 1980), which contains Blount's introduction.

2. Robert W. Creamer, "The Games People Watch," *New York Times Book Review,* 1 December 1974, 90.

3. Phil Musick, "Steeler 'Bricks' Foundation for Good Book," *Pittsburgh Press,* 28 July 1974, D-6.

4. Mike Tharp, "The Boys of Autumn: Three Versions," *Wall Street Journal,* 8 November 1974, 10.

5. John Schulian, "Jocks Are People, Too," *Baltimore Sun,* 1 January 1975, D-4.

6. Jonathan Yardley, "Ringing Out the Old Year—and Reveling in Its Reading," *Sports Illustrated,* 2 December 1974, 12; Yardley, "The Ten Best Sports Books," *Washington Post Book World,* 18 July 1982, 13.

Chapter Five

1. Hugh Sidey, "Assessing a Presidency," *Time,* 18 August 1980, 10.

2. Ibid., 11.

3. Richard Brookhiser, "Feuding in the Rear Guard," *National Review,* 17 October 1980, 1022. In his speech accepting the Republican presidential nomination in 1964, Goldwater said, echoing Thomas Paine in *The Rights of Man,* "Extremism in the defense of liberty is no vice. Moderation . . . in the pursuit of justice is no virtue."

4. Boris Weintraub, "Why Is This Man Laughing? Our Humorists Wonder," *Washington Star,* 8 November 1977, D-1.

5. Gene Hendrix [letter], "Liberal with Accent," *Atlanta Constitution,* 17 August 1976, 5-A; [unsigned], "Ronnie's T-Shirts Rib 'Supertooth,'" *Atlanta Constitution,* 19 August 1976, 17-A. Network quote is from author's recollections.

6. Paul H. Elovitz, "Three Days in Plains," in *Jimmy Carter and Amer-*

ican Fantasy: Psychohistorical Explorations, ed. Lloyd deManse and Henry Ebel (New York: Two Continents/Psychohistory Press, 1977), 44–45.

7. Sally Quinn, "Where Did All the Good Times Go?," *Washington Post,* 18 December 1977, G-1. Quinn's comments were repeated by Richard Reeves in his media report. Cf. "White House Unsociability," *Esquire,* 1 March 1978, 130.

8. Ed Walsh, "Pool Report #9, Air Force One-Beaumont to Waco, Texas," 22 October 1980, Blount Papers.

9. Rick Hertzberg to Roy Blount, Jr., 24 October 1980, Blount Papers.

10. Anatole Broyard, "A Georgia Boy's Blues," *New York Times,* 27 September 1980, 15.

11. Charles Simmons, "People from Georgia and Nearby Places," *New York Times Book Review,* 28 September 1980, 3.

12. Harry Crews, "Laughing through Georgia," *Washington Post Book World,* 28 September 1980, 3.

13. Charles Culhane, "Possum Fair," *National Review,* 19 February 1982, 181–82.

14. *Booklist,* 1 September 1980, 6; *Publishers Weekly,* 22 August 1980, 40.

15. Donald Morrison, "Fine Red Dirt," *Time,* 20 October 1980, 102.

16. Gene Lyons, "Voices of Nothingness," *Nation,* 6 December 1980, 617.

17. Spencer Brown, "Between Journalism and the Essay," *Sewanee Review* 89(Summer 1981):437.

18. Thomas N. Bethel, "Political Book Notes: *Crackers,*" *Washington Monthly,* September 1980, 60.

Chapter Six

1. A. J. Anderson, "Humor," *Library Journal,* 15 September 1982, 1755. Although at least one other area reviewer did not like a Blount book (see Annie Davis, note 8), Blount has enjoyed a good press in New England, as interviews and reviews elsewhere in this chapter indicate.

2. Christopher Lehmann-Haupt, "Books of the Times," *New York Times,* 1 November 1982, C-20; Cathleen Schine, "Baseball, Socks, Sex, and Laughs," *Nation,* 20 November 1982, 540.

3. Telephone conversation with author, 13 June 1989.

4. Telephone conversation with author, 31 May 1989.

5. Nancy A. Walker, *A Very Serious Thing: Women's Humor and American Culture* (Minneapolis: University of Minnesota Press, 1988), 165–66.

6. D. C. Denison, "The Interview: Roy Blount, Jr.," *Boston Globe Magazine,* 23 April 1989, 10.

7. Sigmund Freud, "Humor" ["*Der Humour*"], in *The Future of an Illusion, Civilization and Its Discontents, and Other Works*, vol. 21 of *The Standard Edition of the Complete Psychological Works of Sigmund Freud*, trans. and ed. James Trachey with Anna Freud (London: Hogarth Press and the Institute of Psycho-Analysis, 1961), 161.

8. Annie Davis, "Humor," *Library Journal*, 1 June 1984, 1129–30.

9. Anatole Broyard, "Wit's Temporary Relief," *New York Times*, 28 April 1984, 14.

10. Dan Greenburg, "On Southerners, Salaries and 'Fih," *New York Times Book Review*, 13 May 1984, 12.

11. Ron Givens, "Truly Tasteful Humor," *Newsweek*, 17 September 1984, 82-B.

12. Leslie Bennetts, "Roy Blount Jr. Puts His Misadventures on the Stage," *New York Times*, 25 January 1988, C-17.

13. Craig Horowitz, "Blount Humor," *M*, October 1983, 286. Blount makes this point in several interviews.

14. Letter to author, 20 May 1989.

15. Telephone conversation with author, 12 June 1989.

16. "To Mr. Burrough of St. Louis," in *Mark Twain's Letters*, vol. 1, arranged with comment by Albert Bigelow Paine (New York and London: Harper & Brothers, 1917), 289–91.

17. Mordecai Richler, ed., *The Best of Modern Humor* (New York: Knopf, 1984).

18. Colin McEnroe, "No Doubt of Blount's Talent in 'Not Exactly,'" *Hartford Courant*, 24 November 1985, G-3.

19. Patrick F. McManus, "The Drip-Drip-Drip of Mirth," *New York Times Book Review*, 17 November 1985, 14.

20. Deborah Mason, "Blackened Red Dirt and Other Delicacies," *New York Times Book Review*, 2 April 1989, 9.

21. Peter Keepnews, "Things Have Gotten Silly," *New York Times Book Review*, 2 April 1989, 9.

Chapter Seven

1. Cf. Howard Winston Smith, "An Annotated Edition of Hooper's *Some Adventures of Captain Simon Suggs*," Ph.D. diss., Vanderbilt University, 1965, xiii–ix. Clemens's attitude toward Mark Twain is discussed in most studies of his life and works; the aspect of entrapment within the role is stated clearly and convincingly by James M. Cox in *Mark Twain: The Fate of Humor* (Princeton, N.J.: Princeton University Press, 1966).

2. Brom Weber, "The Misspellers," in *The Comic Imagination in American Literature*, ed. Louis D. Rubin, Jr. (New Brunswick, N.J.: Rutgers University Press, 1973), 127.

3. For a discussion of theories and theorists dealing with this aspect of

humor, see Holland, *Laughing: A Psychology of Humor.* Social aspects and laugh tracks are discussed on pp. 67–68, 81–82.

4. Letter to author, 31 May 1989.

5. Telephone conversation with author, 29 June 1989.

6. Telephone conversation with author, 27 June 1989.

7. Letter to author, 31 May 1989.

8. Rosalie Miller, Minnesota Public Radio, telephone conversation with author, 30 June 1989.

9. Comments on the stage show are based on audiotapes of the 5 February and 6 February 1988 "Roy Blount's Happy Hour and a Half" performances, supplied by Blount to the author.

10. "Who's Who in the Cast," *Playbill,* February 1988, 32; Edith Oliver, "The Theatre: Off-Broadway," *New Yorker,* 16 June 1986, 108.

11. Telephone conversation with author, 27 June 1989.

12. Bennetts, "Roy Blount Jr. Puts His Misadventures on the Stage," C-17.

13. Mel Gussow, "Stage: Roy Blount in Humorists' Series," *New York Times,* 26 January 1988, C-17.

14. Leo Seligsohn, "Sly Country Humor on the City Stage," *Newsday,* 29 January 1988, C-20.

15. David Hinckley, "Roy's a Wry Wrapper," *Daily News,* 27 January 1988, 35.

16. Letter to author, 31 May 1989.

17. Blount, "The Many Faces of Gilda," *Rolling Stone,* 2 November 1978, 44–48.

18. Lamar Alexander, "Blount 'Rumbles' His Way through Hilarious Book," *Nashville Banner,* 8 April 1989, D-10.

19. For a summary and comment on the incident, see [unsigned], "An Oddsmaker's Odd Views," *Sports Illustrated,* 25 January 1988, 7.

20. *Roy Blount, Jr. Reading Crackers, One Fell Soup, and Interview with Roy Blount, Jr.,* interview by Kay Bonetti (Columbia, Mo.: American Audio Prose Library, 1983), sound cassette; *Not Exactly What I Had in Mind* (Auburn, Calif.: The Audio Partners, 1986), two sound cassettes. An audiotape interview with Blount is also included in the "New Letters on the Air" series, produced at the University of Missouri-Kansas City, 1989.

21. Mason, "Blackened Red Dirt and Other Delicacies," 9.

22. Letter to author, 13 June 1989.

Chapter Eight

1. Kingsley Amis, ed. *The New Oxford Book of English Light Verse* (New York: Oxford University Press, 1978), viii.

2. Morris Bishop, "Light Verse in America," in *The Comic Imagination in American Literature,* 259–73.

3. "Don't Anybody Steal These: From My Notebooks over the Last Few Years," *Antaeus* 61 (Autumn 1988):54.

4. The poem is anthologized in *Sweet and Sour: An Anthology of Comic Verse,* ed. Christopher Logue (London: B. T. Batsford, 1983), 170, and in *A Picnic of Poetry: Poems about Food and Drink,* selected by Anne Harvey (London: Blackie and Son, 1988), 49.

5. "Gutes and Eulas," in *Light Year '87,* ed. Robert Wallace (Cleveland, Ohio: Bits Press, 1986), 50–51.

6. Daniel Pinkwater, *"Soupsongs and Webster's Ark,"* *New York Times Book Review,* 7 February 1988, 20.

7. See Ralph Novak, "Picks ands Pans," *People,* 23 November 1987, n.p.; Bruce Cook, "Blount Adds Dash of Nash to Verse-Happy 'Soupsongs,'" [Los Angeles] *Daily News,* 27 March 1988, 27; Colin Covert, "A Look at Strange, Questing Mind of Roy Blount Jr.," *Minneapolis Star Tribune,* 21 November 1987, 1-C.

8. Wayne Greenhaw, "Author Just May Be Funniest U.S. Writer," *Montgomery Advertiser and Alabama Journal,* 26 September 1987, 2-B; Frank Gannon, "Blount Finds Poetic Justice in Back-to-Back Books," *Atlanta Journal-Constitution,* 25 October 1987, 11-J.

9. "A Christmas Carol (for the 80's)," *New York Times,* 19 December 1988, A-17.

10. Letter to author, 13 June 1989.

11. *Writer's Market,* ed. Glenda Tennant Neff (Cincinnati, Ohio: Writer's Digest, 1989), 285.

12. "The Un-British Crossword Puzzle," *Spy,* October 1986, 62.

13. "The Un-British Crossword Puzzle," *Spy,* September 1987, 80.

14. "The Un-British Crossword Puzzle," *Spy,* November 1987, 93.

15. "The Un-British Crossword Puzzle," *Spy,* August 1988, 149.

16. "The Un-British Crossword Puzzle," *Spy,* September 1988, 144.

17. "The Un-British Crossword Puzzle," *Spy,* November 1988, 142.

18. "The Un-British Crossword Puzzle," *Spy,* March 1989, 114.

19. "The Un-British Crossword Puzzle," *Spy,* February 1989, 106.

20. "The Un-British Crossword Puzzle," *Spy,* March 1989, 114.

21. "The Un-British Crossword Puzzle," *Spy,* April 1989, 157.

22. "The Un-British Crossword Puzzle," *Spy,* May 1989, 124.

23. "The Un-British Crossword Puzzle," *Spy,* June 1989, 127.

24. "The Un-British Crossword Puzzle," *Spy,* July 1989, 121.

25. "Introduction" to A.J. Liebling, *The Telephone Booth Indian,* submitted by Blount to North Point Press, Berkeley, California. Manuscript of the introduction supplied by Blount.

Selected Bibliography

PRIMARY WORKS

Books

About Three Bricks Shy of a Load: A Highly Irregular Lowdown on the Year the Pittsburgh Steelers Were Super but Missed the Bowl. Boston: Little, Brown, 1974; New York: Ballantine Books, 1980.

Crackers: This Whole Many-Angled Thing of Jimmy, More Carters, Ominous Little Animals, Sad Singing Women, My Daddy and Me. New York: Knopf, 1980; Ballantine Books, 1982.

First Hubby. New York: Villard, 1990.

It Grows on You: The Hair-Raising Story of Human Plumage. New York: Doubleday, 1986.

Not Exactly What I Had in Mind. Boston: Atlantic Monthly Press, 1985; New York: Penguin, 1985.

Now, Where Were We? New York: Villard, 1989.

One Fell Soup, or I'm Just a Bug on the Windshield of Life. Boston: Little, Brown, 1982; New York: Penguin, 1984.

Soupsongs/Webster's Ark. Boston: Houghton Mifflin, 1987.

What Men Don't Tell Women. Boston: Atlantic Monthly Press, 1984; New York: Penguin, 1985.

Magazine Pieces

Entries are listed chronologically. Page number is where article begins.

In *Sports Illustrated*
"A Paper Tiger Wins with Steel." 5 August 1968, 46.
"The Big Zinger from Binger." 31 March 1969, 26.
"Guess Who's Coming Up?" 23 June 1969, 48.
"A Torrid Time for the Twins." 21 July 1969, 16.
"A New Slant on an Old Game in Atlanta." 1 September 1969, 40.
"Yo Yo Yo, Rowa Hu Rowa, Hru Hru." 17 April 1972, 50.
"Knock 'Im Out, Jay-ree!" 30 April 1973, 74.
"I'm the Type of Swimmer Lifeguards Hate." 18 June 1973, 36.
"Attacking the Amazon." 13 April 1987, 60.

In *Spy,* "The Un-British Crossword Puzzle"
October 1986, 62.
September 1987, 70.

November 1987, 93.
August 1988, 149.
September 1988, 144.
November 1988, 142.
February 1989, 106.
March 1989, 114.
April 1989, 157.
May 1989, 124.
June 1989, 127.
July 1989, 121.

Miscellaneous

"Pistol Pete Is up against the Pros," under pseudonym Noah Sanders. *New York Times Magazine,* 11 October 1970, 32.

"'Nobody Does Anything Better Than Me in Baseball,' Says Roberto Clemente . . . Well, He's Right," under pseudonym C. R. Ways. *New York Times Magazine,* 9 April 1972, 38.

"For the Record." *New Yorker,* 29 April 1974, 42.

"Whose Who?" *New Yorker* 54 (14 August 1978), 28.

"The Many Faces of Gilda." *Rolling Stone,* 2 November 1978, 44.

"Who's Who in the Cast." *Playbill,* February 1988, 32.

"Adventures in the Demme Monde." *Esquire,* September 1988, 207.

Essays in Anthologies and Literary Journals

Entries are listed chronologically.

"Frozen Leopard: Hemingway and the Code." Spectrum 1 (Fall 1962):22–28.

"Adrift in a School of Sharks and Other Uneasy Circumstances." *Spectrum* 1(Spring 1963):47–49.

"Shaw and Comedy—Fire and Ice and Some Interesting Things in Between." *Spectrum* 2(Fall 1963):28–34.

"Trash No More," from *Crackers.* In *The Best of Modern Humor,* edited by Mordecai Richler. New York: Knopf, 1984. The anthology that Blount discussed in "What's So Humorous?" in *Not Exactly What I Had in Mind.* Richler calls Blount "one of the most talented of the new American humorists."

"Gutes and Eulas." In *Light Year '87,* edited by Robert Wallace. Cleveland, Ohio: Bits Press, 1986.

"Don't Anybody Steal These: From My Notebooks over the Last Few Years." *Antaeus* 61(Autumn 1988):46–56.

"Amazon Adventure." In *Paths Less Travelled,* edited by Richard Bangs and Christian Kallen. New York: Atheneum, 1988. A longer version of "Attacking the Amazon."

"Song against Broccoli." In *A Picnic of Poetry: Poems about Food and Drink,* edited by Anne Harvey. London: Blackie and Son, Ltd., 1988.   .

"Song against Broccoli." In *Sweet and Sour: An Anthology of Comic Verse*, edited by Christopher Logue. London: B. T. Batsford, 1983.

Newspaper Pieces

Entries are listed chronologically. Page number is where article begins.

In the *Vanderbilt Hustler*

"Chancellor's Chapel Talk Asks Proper Breadth in Education." 2 October 1959, 1.

"Senate Endorses Oust of Lawson Unanimously, Passes New Constitution." 11 March 1960, 1.

"'No Position' Taken on Yates by 'V.'" 15 April 1960, 1.

"VU Students Have Access to Coffee House Atmosphere (18 Kinds) at 'Tulip Is Black.'" 30 September 1960, 1.

"John Crowe Ransom to Return Next Fall." 10 February 1961, 1.

"VU Humor Magazine Has Long, Unhappy Past." 3 March 1961, 1.

"Porter Reads 'Jilting,' Warren Speaks to Highlight VU Literary Symposium." 28 April 1961, 1.

"Out with Curry, in with Law School; Squirrel Water Situation Called Critical." 19 May 1961, 1.

"John Crowe Ransom 'At Home with Everybody,' to Close Out Teaching Career after Long Absence." 29 September 1961, 1.

"We're Nice, Normal Enough; No Twirlers in Slacks Needed." 29 September 1961, 4.

"'Male Animal' Does for Professors What Even 'Seminar Six' Wouldn't." 20 October 1961, 1.

"There's Not Any Bunk in UGF, Says the 32-inch Poem of Mr. S." 2 November 1961, 4.

"Enter Sanders with a Few Words on Conservatism, and Coed Shorts." 10 November 1961, 4.

"Stabbing, Pizza Mark Ride with Police." 8 December 1961, 1.

"Touchy Composition in Black and White." 12 January 1962, 4.

"On Intellectual Climate, and Bettering It." 2 March 1962, 4.

"Of Time and Place, and Smugness of Race." 20 April 1962, 4.

"Of Chancellor, Bias, Art, Laughter, Aix." 11 May 1962, 4.

"Maria Beale Fletcher Wants to Forget Miss America and 'Just Be Me.'" 14 September 1962, 1.

"The Sound of Music." 14 September 1962, 4.

"Coolidge on Rush: 'Don't.'" 28 September 1962, 4.

"The Silent Senate." 12 October 1962, 4.

"Arguing and the Senate." 19 October 1962, 4.

"South Forgets Its Own Values." 19 October 1962, 4.

"You Can't Go Home Again." 16 November 1962, 4.

"More Attorney and Less General." 30 November 1962, 4.

"Some of Our Best Friends" 7 December 1962, 4.

"Is Your Daddy Greek?" 15 February 1963, 4.
"Two Alums and Their Different Books." 26 April 1963, 4.

In the *Atlanta Journal*
"With Reservations in Reserve." 22 June 1967, 15-B.
"Whatever Happened to Socks." 12 July, 1967, 17-B.
"Ours Is Just to Reason Why." 19 December 1967, 7.
"You Wouldn't Say 'Nigroo Power.'" 29 February 1968, 23-A.
"Compare Agrarians, Black Power." 7 May 1968, 17-A.
"Davidson: Whole in His Acts." 9 May 1968, 21-A.

Miscellaneous
"A Christmas Carol (for the 80's). *New York Times,* 19 December 1988, A-17.

Correspondence

Letters to Jerry Elijah Brown, 13 October 1988; 17, 20, 31 May 1989; 13
      June 1989; 18, 28 July 1989.
Letter to Charles J. Cella, 14 March 1986. Special Collections, Jean and Alex-
      ander Heard Library, Vanderbilt University, Nashville, Tennessee.

Tapes and Audiocassettes

Roy Blount Jr. Reading Crackers, One Fell Soup, and Interview with Roy Blount Jr.
      Interview by Kay Bonnetti. Columbia, Mo.: American Audio Prose Li-
      brary, 1983. Sound cassette.
Not Exactly What I Had in Mind. Auburn, Calif.: The Audio Partners, 1986.
      Two sound cassettes.
Audiotape of "Roy Blount Jr.'s Happy Hour and a Half" (5 and 6 February
      1988) provided to author by Blount.
Interview with Roy Blount Jr. "New Letters on the Air." Kansas City: University
      of Missouri, 1989.

Miscellaneous

"Introduction," prepared for A.J. Liebling's *The Telephone Booth Indian.* Blount
      Papers.

SECONDARY WORKS

Books and Parts of Books about Blount's Genre

Amis, Kingsley, ed. *The New Oxford Book of English Light Verse.* New York:
      Oxford University Press, 1978. Introduction sets light verse in its proper
      context without making the whole idea burdensome.

Aristotle. *The "Art" of Rhetoric.* Translated by John Henry Freeze. Cambridge, Mass.: Harvard University Press; London: Heinemann, 1959. Raises the notion that humor derives from incongruity; introduces the concept of wit.

"Blount, Roy (Alton), Jr." In *Contemporary Authors, New Revision Series,* vol. 10. Detroit, Mich.: Gale Research, 1983.

Cox, James M. *Mark Twain: The Fate of Humor.* Princeton, N.J.: Princeton University Press, 1966. Elevates humor as a serious form of American writing and demonstrates that it was the essential mode for Clemens. Useful in comparing Blount and other writers with the nation's most successful literary humorist.

Elovitz, Paul H. "Three Days in Plains." In *Jimmy Carter and American Fantasy: Psychohistorical Explorations,* edited by Lloyd deManse and Henry Ebel. New York: Two Continents/Psychohistory Press, 1977. An unintentionally funny attempt by five psychohistorians to understand the Carter phenomenon.

Freud, Sigmund. "Humor" ["Der Humor"]. In *The Future of an Illusion, Civilization and Its Discontents, and Other Works,* translated and edited by James Trachey and Anna Freud. Vol. 21, *The Standard Edition of the Complete Psychological Works of Sigmund Freud.* London: Hogarth Press and the Institute of Psycho-Analysis, 1961. Written in 1927, the essay follows Freud's analysis in *Jokes* (1903) and relates humor to his final conception of the human psyche.

Holland, Norman. *Laughing: A Psychology of Humor.* Ithaca, N.Y., and London: Cornell University Press, 1982. A lucid survey of critical theory from Aristotle to the present, followed by the author's theory.

Robison, Carson J. "Life Gits Tee-Jus, Don't It?" In *Sing Your Heart Out, Country Boy,* edited by Dorothy Horstman. Nashville: Country Music Foundation, 1986. The white minstrel poem that Blount recited as a child. Some stanzas also are in lyrics to the song "I'm Busted."

Rubin, Louis D., Jr., ed. *The Comic Imagination in American Literature.* New Brunswick, N.J.: Rutgers University Press, 1973. Essays by James M. Cox, Brom Weber, and Morris Bishop are especially helpful in understanding Blount as a serious writer, literary comedian, and light verse poet.

Smith, Howard Winston. "An Annotated Edition of Hooper's *Some Adventures of Captain Simon Suggs.*" Ph.D. diss., Vanderbilt University, 1965. Should be published; introduction is best the existing preparation for a general understanding of the practice and politics of frontier Southern American humor.

Twain, Mark. *Mark Twain's Letters,* arranged with comment by Albert Bigelow Paine. Vol. 1, pp. 289–91. New York and London: Harper & Brothers, 1917. Letters reveal similarities between Clemens and Blount, who quotes from one of the letters ("To Mr. Burrough of St. Louis") in

"Who's the Funniest American Writer?" in *Not Exactly What I Had in Mind.*

White, E. B., and Katharine S. White. *A Subtreasury of American Humor.* New York: Coward-McCann, 1941. Strongly influenced by the *New Yorker* humorists, read by Roy Blount as a teenager, and remembered for its impact on his life.

Books Referring to Blount's Humor

Encyclopedia of Southern Culture. Edited by Charles Reagan Wilson and William Ferris. Chapel Hill, N.C., and London: University of North Carolina Press, 1989. Blount referred to under several headings for his comments on possums, grits, regional types; he is also called "one of the preeminent Southern interpreters of the Carters."

Reed, John Shelton. *Southern Folk, Plain & Fancy: Native White Social Types.* Athens and London: University of Georgia Press, 1986. Illustrates that profound social analysis and humor are not mutually exclusive; the author values Blount's perceptions of the way ethnic labels ("good old boy," "hillbilly") are applied to white Southerners and ends the book with Blount's statement from "The Lowdown on Southern Hospitality": "Southerners get a charge out of being typical."

Walker, Nancy A. *A Very Serious Thing: Women's Humor and American Culture.* Minneapolis: University of Minnesota Press, 1988. Views contemporary humor from a feminist perspective and sees Blount as resisting "gender equality."

Article and Reviews in Periodicals

Page number is where article begins.

Anderson, A. J. "Humor." *Library Journal,* 15 September 1982, 1755.

Bethel, Thomas N. "Political Book Notes: *Crackers.*" *Washington Monthly,* September 1980, 60.

Brookhiser, Richard. "Feuding in the Rear Guard." *National Review,* 17 October 1980, 1022.

Brown, Spencer. "Between Journalism and the Essay." *Sewanee Review* 89(Summer 1981):437.

"Crackers." *Booklist,* 1 September 1980, 6.

"Crackers." *Publishers Weekly,* 22 August 1980, 40.

Creamer, Robert W. "The Games People Watch." *New York Times Book Review,* 1 December 1974, 90.

Crews, Harry. "Laughing through Georgia." *Washington Post Book World,* 28 September 1980, 3.

Culhane, Charles. "Possum Fair." *National Review,* 19 February 1982, 181.

Davis, Annie. "Humor." *Library Journal,* 1 June 1984, 1129.

Denison, D. C. "The Interview: Roy Blount, Jr." *Boston Globe Magazine,* 23 April 1989, 8.

Epstein, Joseph. "Sid, You Made the Prose Too Thin." *Commentary* 84(September 1987):53.

"Esquire's Irksome Quirks," *Columbia Journalism Review,* September/October 1982, 16.

Givens, Ron. "Truly Tasteful Humor." *Newsweek,* 17 September 1984, 82-B.

Greenburg, Dan. "On Southerners, Salaries and 'Fih.'" *New York Times Book Review,* 18 May 1984, 12.

Horowitz, Craig. "Blount Humor." *M,* October 1983, 286.

Keepnews, Peter. "Things Have Gotten Silly." *New York Times Book Review,* 2 April 1989, 9.

Kloer, Phil. "The Blount Truth." *Atlanta Weekly,* 29 March 1987, 6.

Lyons, Gene. "Voices of Nothingness." *Nation,* 6 December 1980, 617.

Mason, Deborah. "Blackened Red Dirt and Other Delicacies." *New York Times Book Review,* 2 April 1989, 9.

McManus, Patrick F. "The Drip-Drip-Drip of Mirth." *New York Times Book Review,* 17 November 1985, 14.

Morrison, Donald. "Fine Red Dirt." *Time,* 20 October 1980, 102.

Novak, Ralph. "Picks and Pans." *People,* 23 November 1987, n.p. "An Odds-maker's Odd Views." *Sports Illustrated,* 25 January 1988, 7.

Oliver, Edith. "The Theatre: Off-Broadway." *New Yorker,* 16 June 1986, 108.

Penrice, Daniel. "Blount-edged Humor." *Boston Globe Sunday Magazine,* 17 June 1984, 35.

Pinkwater, Daniel. *"Soupsongs* and *Webster's Ark." New York Times Book Review,* 7 February 1988, 20.

Reeves, Richard. "What House Unsociability." *Esquire,* 1 March 1978, 128, 130.

Rosen, Richard. "Heirs to Maxwell Perkins." *Horizon,* April 1981, 50.

Schine, Cathleen. "Baseball, Socks, Sex and Laughs." *Nation,* 20 November 1982, 539.

Sidey, Hugh. "Assessing a Presidency." *Time,* 18 August 1980, 10.

Simmons, Charles. "People from Georgia and Nearby Places." *New York Times Book Review,* 28 September 1980, 15.

Yardley, Jonathan. "Ringing Out the Old Year—and Reveling in Its Reading." *Sports Illustrated,* 2 December 1974, 12.

———. "The Ten Best Sports Books." *Washington Post Book World,* 18 July 1982, 13, 17.

Newspaper Articles

Page number is where article begins.

Aden, John M. "Professors, Students Comment on Sit-in Controversy." *Vanderbilt Hustler,* 11 January 1963, 10.

Alexander, Lamar. "Blount 'Rumbles' His Way through Hilarious Book." *Nashville Banner,* 8 April 1989, D-10.

"Alexander V-Book Head; Blount Is Associate Editor." *Vanderbilt Hustler,* 21 April 1961, 1.

Barrett, Lionel. "Senate President Breaks Silence, Hits 'H' Misconception, Typos." *Vanderbilt Hustler,* 19 October 1962, 5.

Bennetts, Leslie. "Roy Blount Jr. Puts His Misadventures on the Stage." *New York Times,* 25 January 1988, C-17.

"Blount Ends Term with Press Blast." *Atlanta Constitution,* 29 December 1972, 18-A.

"A Blount Reply." *Pittsburgh Post-Gazette,* 11 September 1982, 6.

Broyard, Anatole. "A Georgia Boy's Blues." *New York Times,* 27 September 1980, 15.

————. "Wit's Temporary Relief." *New York Times,* 28 April 1984, 14.

Chapin, Kim. "Under Sharp Lens of a Native Son, Carter Falls Short." *Atlanta Journal-Constitution,* 9 November 1980, E-2.

Cook, Bruce. "Blount Adds Dash of Nash to Verse-Happy *Soupsongs.*" [Los Angeles] *Daily News,* 27 March 1988, 27.

Covert, Colin. "A Look at [the] Strange, Questing Mind of Roy Blount, Jr." *Minneapolis Star Tribune,* 21 November 1987, 1-C.

"Editor Daughtrey Promises Humor in Next Year's 'Vagabond' Issues." *Vanderbilt Hustler,* 12 May 1961, 1.

Foster, Jim. "ODK Taps Six Junior Leaders." *Vanderbilt Hustler,* 18 May 1962, 1.

Gannon, Frank. "Blount Finds Poetic Justice in Back-to-Back Books." *Atlanta Journal-Constitution,* 25 October 1987, 11-J.

Greenhaw, Wayne. "Author Just May Be Funniest U.S. Writer." *Montgomery Advertiser and Alabama Journal,* 26 September 1987, 2-B.

Gussow, Mel. "Stage: Roy Blount in Humorists' Series." *New York Times,* 26 January 1988, C-17.

Hendrix, Gene. "Liberal with Accent" [letter]. *Atlanta Constitution,* 17 August 1976, 5-A.

Hinckley, David. "Roy's a Wry Wrapper." [Los Angeles] *Daily News,* 27 January 1988, 35.

"Hustler, Other College Publications Explode in Nationwide Headlines." *Vanderbilt Hustler,* 3 May 1963, 2.

Lehmann-Haupt, Christopher. "Books of the Times." *New York Times,* 1 November 1982, C-20.

McEnroe, Colin. "No Doubt of Blount's Talent in 'Not Exactly.'" *Hartford Courant,* 24 November 1985, 63.

Monk, Diane. "'Regenerated' Vagabond to Have Balance of Humor, Prose, Poetry." *Vanderbilt Hustler,* 16 February 1962, 5.

Musick, Phil. "Steeler 'Bricks' Foundation for Good Book." *Pittsburgh Press,* 28 July 1974, D-6.

Quinn, Sally. "Where Did All the Good Times Go?" *Washington Post,* 18 December 1977, G-1.
"Roy A. Blount: S & L President." *Atlanta Constitution,* 17 April 1974, 14-A.
"Roy A. Blount, Sr." *Atlanta Constitution,* 18 April 1974, 4-A.
"Ronnie's T-shirts Rib 'Supertooth.'" *Atlanta Constitution,* 19 August 1976, 17-A.
Schulian, John. "Jocks Are People, Too." *Baltimore Sun,* 1 January 1975, D-4.
Seligsohn, Leo. "Sly Country Humor on the City Stage." *Newsday,* 29 January 1988, C-20.
Tharp, Mike. "The Boys of Autumn: Three Versions." *Wall Street Journal,* 8 November 1974, 10.
Weintraub, Boris. "Why Is This Man Laughing? Our Humorists Wonder." *Washington Star,* 8 November 1977, D-1.

Miscellaneous

Ackermann-Blount, Joan. Telephone conversation with author, 19 July 1989.
Blount, Susan. Telephone conversation with author, 27 March 1989.
Cleghorn, Reese. Telephone interview with author, 5 April 1989.
Hertzberg, Rick. Letter to Roy Blount, Jr., 24 October 1980. Blount Papers.
Miller, Rosalie (Minnesota Public Radio). Telephone conversation with author, 30 June 1989.
Personnel files. *Atlanta Journal-Constitution,* Atlanta, Georgia.
Walsh, Ed. "Pool Report #9, Air Force One—Beaumont to Waco, Texas." 22 October 1980. Blount Papers.

Index